M000190450

Irene C. Fountas & Gay Su Pinnell

# Sing a Song of
# Poetry

Irene C. Fountas & Gay Su Pinnell

# Sing a Song of
# Poetry

## A Teaching Resource for Phonemic Awareness, Phonics, and Fluency

**Grade 1**

## Revised Edition

**HEINEMANN**
Portsmouth, NH

**Heinemann**

361 Hanover Street

Portsmouth, NH 03801–3912

www.heinemann.com

*Offices and agents throughout the world*

© 2018 by Irene C. Fountas and Gay Su Pinnell

All rights reserved. No part of this book may be reproduced in any form or by any electronic or mechanical means, including information storage and retrieval systems, without permission in writing from the publisher, except by a reviewer, who may quote brief passages in a review; and with the exception of reproducibles (identified by the *Sing a Song of Poetry* copyright line), which may be photocopied for classroom use.

*The authors have dedicated a great deal of time and effort to writing the content of this book, and their written expression is protected by copyright law. We respectfully ask that you do not adapt, reuse, or copy anything on third-party (whether for-profit or not-for-profit) lesson-sharing websites. As always, we're happy to answer any questions you may have.*

**—Heinemann Publishers**

"Dedicated to Teachers" is a trademark of Greenwood Publishing Group, Inc.

Cataloging-in-Publication Data is on file at the Library of Congress.

ISBN-13: 978-0-325-09295-9
Previously published under ISBN-13: 978-0-325-00656-7

*Editorial:* Kimberly Capriola, David Pence
*Production:* Hilary Goff
*Cover and interior designs:* Monica Ann Crigler
*Typesetter:* Gina Poirier Design
*Manufacturing:* Erin St. Hilaire

Printed in the United States of America on acid-free paper
22  21  20  19  18  VP  1  2  3  4  5

# Contents

# Poems

## I

Contents

## P

## Q

## R

## S

## T

## U

## V

## W

# Introduction

*Sing a Song of Poetry* rolls off the tongue and moves the heart and spirit, if not the feet and hands. Rhythmical language of any sort delights young children as it surrounds them with the magical sounds of dancing words. But poetry, verse, and song provide the magic of teaching as well; indeed, oral language is the doorway to the world of written language and the foundation for literacy. As firstgraders respond to the sound patterns, intriguing words, and inspiring ideas they find in poems, songs, and rhymes, they are learning invaluable lessons about the ways in which our language works—knowledge that will serve them well as they become readers and writers.

The poems, songs, and rhymes in this volume are a rich source of language, ideas, and imagery that will help firstgraders use and enjoy oral and written language. This volume is a companion to the lessons described in *The Fountas & Pinnell Phonics, Spelling, and Word Study Lessons, Grade 1* (2018). It can also be used as a stand-alone resource for language and literacy opportunities in any early childhood or primary classroom.

Jack, be nimble,
Jack, be quick,
Jack, jump over
The candlestick.

*A poem illustrated by a child in an Apply activity*

Experiences with poetry help children become aware of the phonological system of language and provide a foundation for matching sounds with letters, letter clusters, and word parts. You can use poems, chants, and songs to help children

- listen for and identify rhyming words;
- connect words that have the same beginning, ending, or medial sound;
- begin to match sounds to letters in words;
- introduce the culture, traditional language, and rhythmic patterns of nursery rhymes;
- stimulate and enrich language development;
- promote phonemic awareness by helping them notice words; syllables; rhymes; onsets and rimes; and beginning, ending, and medial sounds;
- enhance oral language use in articulate ways;
- instill an appreciation of poetry and prose;
- build vocabulary;
- experience meaningful print and learn early reading behaviors (e.g., directionality, word-by-word matching);
- participate in fluent, phrased reading;
- build meaningful concepts about print (letters, words, punctuation);
- introduce letters and set the scene for letter recognition; and
- provide a base from which to explore writing.

Once a poem is introduced in your classroom, it has multiple uses for teaching. Below are some examples.

- Reread the poem to have children highlight rhyming words with highlighter tape.
- Reread the poem with sticky notes over rhyming words so children can predict.
- Cover all but the first letter of several words, and have children predict and then check them as you reread.
- Have children highlight any features of words that they are studying: e.g., first letters, onsets, rimes, and endings.
- Cover names in the poem with sticky notes and substitute with children's names.
- Give children a small version of the poem that they can glue in a personal poetry book and then illustrate.
- During independent work time, let children read their personal poetry book with a partner.
- During independent work time, children can read the chart with a partner.

In addition to activities like those above, read the suggestions in small print at the bottom of each poem. They describe ways you can work with the poem—sometimes adding verses or changing them.

Young children love poetry with rhythm and rhyme; the language of poetry sings inside their heads. As they grow older, they will learn to appreciate poetry without rhyme, but rhymes and songs are the staple of early childhood and for good reason.

# Values and Goals of Poetry in First-grade Classrooms

**Poetry expands children's oral language abilities as it:**
- provides texts that are easy to remember;
- builds a repertoire of the unique patterns and forms of language;
- helps children become sensitive to and enjoy the sounds of language—rhymes, alliteration, assonance, onomatopoeia (*buzz, whiz, woof*);
- supports articulation and elocution;
- extends listening and speaking vocabularies;
- expands knowledge of the complex syntax of language;
- encourages children to manipulate and play with language;
- develops phonological awareness (rhyme, syllables, onsets and rimes);
- makes it easy for children to isolate and identify sounds, take words apart, and change sounds in words to make new words;
- develops phonemic awareness (the ability to manipulate individual sounds); and
- provides rich examples of comparisons such as similes and metaphors.

**Poetry expands children's written language abilities as it:**
- gives them access to memorable language that they can then match up with print;
- expands spoken vocabulary, making it easier later for them to read words;
- helps them notice aspects of print;
- provides opportunities to learn and recognize words that rhyme, end the same, start the same, or sound the same in the middle;
- helps them begin to notice the letters and letter patterns associated with sounds;
- provides a setting in which to develop the concept of a word and notice how spaces are used to define words in written language; and
- provides models of fluent reading to help children get the feel of it.

**Poetry expands children's content knowledge as it:**
- provides new perceptions and ideas for them to think about;
- helps them develop conceptual understandings;
- encourages them to develop a sense of humor; and
- sensitizes them to the forms and styles of poetry.

**Poetry contributes to children's social knowledge and skills as it:**
- provides artistic and aesthetic experiences;
- creates a sense of community through enjoying rhymes and songs as a group;
- gives them access to English-speaking culture;
- provides a window to many other cultures;
- provides a common language for a group of children to share; and
- creates memories of shared enjoyable times.

Poetry provides resources for the heart and spirit. Immersing children in simple poetry at an early age instills a lifelong habit of enjoying language and seeking out poetry in order to expand our vision. Poetry joins us to the past and to our fellow human beings in the present.

# The Language and Literary Features of Poetry

The following unique elements provide the essence of poetry's appeal. In the poems appropriate for young children, language patterns, rhyme, rhythm, and humor dominate, but all the elements are present.

## Rhyme

Many of the simple poems that children enjoy include words that rhyme. Rhyme is the repetition of the last vowel and consonant sounds in words in verse, especially at the ends of lines. For example, in the poem "Handy Pandy," the words *Jack-a-dandy* and *candy* rhyme because the sounds after the first /d/ in *Jack-a-dandy* are repeated in the second and third syllables of *candy*.

In this book, many of the rhyming words have a single syllable. To understand rhyme in one-syllable words, it's helpful to understand the parts of a syllable. In a syllable, the onset is the part (the consonant, consonant cluster, or consonant digraph) that comes before the vowel. In a syllable, the rime is the ending part containing the letters that represent the vowel sound and the consonant letters that follow. For example, in the one-syllable word *play*, the onset is *pl* and the rime is *ay*. In the word *day*, the onset is *d* and the rime is *ay*. The words *play* and *day* rhyme because they have rimes that sound the same. Remember, two rimes with different spellings (such as *may* and *sleigh*) can rhyme if they have the same sounds.

Consider the poem "Coffee and Tea":

> My sister, Molly, and I fell out,
>
> And what do you think it was about?
>
> She loved coffee and I loved tea,
>
> And that was the reason we couldn't agree.

The words *out* and *about* rhyme because the sounds in the word *out* are repeated in the second syllable of *about*. Likewise, the words *tea* and *agree* rhyme because the rime in the second syllable of *agree* has the same sounds as the rime in the word *tea*. Rhyme is appealing and memorable; rhyme always refers to the sound of the ending part of the word, not necessarily the spelling.

## Rhythm

The beat, or *rhythm*, of poetry brings delight to young children as they chant rhymes and songs in unison, and it helps them remember them. Both rhyme and rhythm make it easy for children to recite, remember, and eventually read words fluently.

For example, consider the poem "I Had a Little Brother":

> I had a little brother
>
> No bigger than my thumb;
>
> I put him in the coffee pot
>
> Where he rattled like a drum.

## Figurative and Archaic Language

As young children internalize poetry, they respond to the sensory images and figurative language. Poetry often uses language that compares two objects or ideas to allow the reader to see something more clearly or understand something in a new way, as in the poem "Snowman":

> There is a snowman as round as a ball.
>
> He has two large eyes, but he's not very tall.
>
> If the sun shines down on him today,
>
> My jolly snowman will melt away.

Often rhymes, chants, and songs contain *onomatopoeia*, which is the representation of sound with words. For example, words like *whoosh* sound like the phenomenon they represent. Consider this example from "Slip on Your Raincoat":

> Slip on your raincoat.
>
> Pull on your galoshes.
>
> Wading in puddles
>
> Making splishes and sploshes.
>
> All around the town.

Poetry often presents children with verses that have been enjoyed for centuries. Sometimes they can internalize archaic language like *porridge* and *candlestick* as they chant and sing. But some archaic concepts may warrant explanation: e.g., rubbing dirty clothes clean like in the poem "The Old Woman," or roosters crowing as an alarm clock. Additionally, old-fashioned language structures and expressions like *shall* and *'twas* in the poem "Lavender's Blue," or *shook with mirth* in the poem "The Man in the Moon" may need to be defined. They are often—though not solely—present in nursery rhymes.

## Language Patterns

Rhymes and poems are enjoyable in large part because of the language patterns that are included. *Alliteration*, the repetition of consonant sounds, is evident in the poem "The Big Black Bug":

> The big black bug
>
> Bit the big black bear
>
> But the big black bear
>
> Bit the big black bug back!

Children love these tongue twisters, and they are an excellent way to help them internalize initial sounds. Another good example is the poem "Fresh Fried Fish":

> Fresh fried fish,
>
> Fresh fish fried,
>
> Fried fresh fish,
>
> Fish fried fresh.

Another common pattern is the repetition of vowel sounds, called *assonance*. For example, the poem "Moon, Moon" repeats /o͞o/:

> Moon, moon,
>
> Silvery spoon,
>
> Floating still,
>
> On a night in June.
>
> Moon, moon,
>
> Back too soon,
>
> White and pale
>
> In the afternoon.

## Repetition

Many poems, particularly songs, have repeating stanzas or phrases. Notice that in the first stanza of the following poem, "The More We Get Together," the word *together* and the line *Oh, the more we get together* are repeated:

> Oh, the more we get together,
>
> Together, together,
>
> Oh, the more we get together,
>
> The happier we'll be.

Rhythmic repetition like this helps children learn these rhymes easily; many have been set to music and can be sung, such as the poem "The Ants Go Marching."

## Sensory Images

Poetry arouses the senses. Just a few words can evoke memories, elicit visual images, point out absurdities, and help us enter unique worlds. For example, children enjoy the nonsense in the nursery rhyme "There Was an Old Lady Who Swallowed a Fly":

> There was an old lady who swallowed a fly.
>
> I don't know why she swallowed the fly.
>
> Perhaps she'll die.
>
> There was an old lady who swallowed a spider
>
> That wriggled and jiggled and tickled inside her.
>
> She swallowed the spider to catch the fly.
>
> I don't know why she swallowed the fly.
>
> Perhaps she'll die.

# Important Areas of Learning for Firstgraders

The most important benefit of using poetry in first-grade classrooms is the facilitation of children's oral language development. Through their involvement in poetry, children expand their knowledge of the vocabulary and syntax of English as well as their sensitivity to the *phonology*, or sounds of the language. In addition, using poetry has profound implications for helping children learn to read and write. See *Guided Reading: Responsive Teaching Across the Grades*, Second Edition (Fountas and Pinnell 2017) and *Word Matters: Teaching Phonics and Spelling in the Reading/Writing Classroom* (Pinnell and Fountas 1998).

Several important areas of learning form a foundation for becoming literate. Even though formal reading instruction began in the second half of kindergarten, young children need to continue developing along all of these dimensions through the early childhood years.

## Phonological Awareness

The phonological system encompasses the sounds of a language. When children hear, chant, or sing poems, they become more aware of sound patterns and how they are connected (for example, words that rhyme or words that start the same). Gradually, they are able to identify the individual sounds (or *phonemes*) in words. *Phonemic awareness,* or the ability to identify individual sounds in words, is essential when children are learning to connect sounds and letters. Young children need to learn to play with language and manipulate sounds. They can

- listen for and identify rhyming words;
- listen for and identify syllables within words;
- listen for and identify onsets and rimes;
- listen for individual sounds in words;
- match words with similar sounds;
- break words into individual sounds (phonemes) and into syllables;
- blend sounds to form words; and
- match sounds and letters.

## Letter Learning

To be able to recognize letters, children need to distinguish the features that make one letter different from every other letter. The differences between letters are sometimes quite small (for example, *h* and *n*), and distinguishing such features requires close attention. Also, orientation makes a difference (for example, *u* and *n*). Learning how to look at letters is essential if children are to connect sounds and letters and and learn letter names. Through repeated exposure to letters in the poems they experience in shared reading, children begin to notice the letters that are embedded in print. They can

- notice and locate letters in words;
- learn to find the beginning letter of a word;
- connect words by beginning or ending letters; and
- connect words in poems to letters in their names.

## Phonics

Teaching children how the sounds of language are connected to the letters (to learn letter-sound relationships) is an instructional approach called *phonics*. Early on, young children will learn the easy-to-hear consonant sounds (beginning or ending) and easy-to-hear vowels (long vowels).

## Concepts About Print

Encounters with poetry will also help children acquire some basic understandings about how print works. For example, the concepts of first and last are important in written language. Children who are just beginning to notice the world of print will have the opportunity to learn that they read from left to right across a line of print and that at the end of the line, you return to the left and again read left to right. One spoken word matches one group of printed letters, and a printed word has a space on each side of it. It is important for children to understand that letters are embedded in print and that they can identify words by the sequence of the letters. They can

- notice print as the carrier of the message in a text;
- follow print from top to bottom and over pages of text;
- follow print left to right in a familiar text;
- return to the left margin at the end of the line;
- locate words by saying them and thinking about the first sound and letter;
- find rhyming words;
- recognize uppercase and lowercase letters;
- locate letters and familiar words in text;
- distinguish between a letter and a word; and
- notice simple punctuation.

## Fluency

Young children will become verbally fluent as they repeat poems and use the phrases, pauses, stresses, and intonation of the language. They will also become more fluent in picking up the print from the page as many words become more automatic and their reading vocabulary expands. They can

- read in phrases;
- use expression;
- stop at periods and pause at commas;
- raise the voice at question marks;
- sound excited at an exclamation mark;
- read smoothly;
- put their words together so it sounds like language;
- vary intonation and stress to reflect meaning; and
- recognize some words quickly.

# Selecting Poetry for Young Children

Selecting poetry for children depends on your purpose. You will want to consider whether they will experience the poems orally or if you will eventually expect them to process the print. Children can listen to and recite more complex poems than they can read. Simple, engaging, repetitive poems will be easy for them to remember. Knowing poems, songs, and rhymes increases children's ability to notice the sounds of language; they learn many new words to add to their oral vocabulary. When they repeat familiar poems, they are using the syntax, or grammar, of written language, which is different from their everyday speech. Experiencing and internalizing this complex language sets the scene for reading and understanding the simple texts they will begin to read as well as the more complex texts they will encounter later.

In shared reading, children will begin to read with you (using an enlarged version of the text that everyone can see). In the process, they will begin to notice characteristics of print. The first poems children encounter in shared reading should

- be relatively short;
- employ repetition and patterned language;
- feature a large number of words that are easy to read;
- present generally simple vocabulary (although children may enjoy many rhymes without knowing the precise meaning of some archaic words, such as *pease porridge*); and
- focus on concepts and ideas that are familiar (for example, visual imagery and metaphor require more of children than simple rhymes and songs).

We recommend that first-grade children have the opportunity to read a large number of poems in this highly supported way. The poems in this book represent a gradient of difficulty. At the beginning of the year, select very simple poems, and then gradually increase the level of challenge. The poems in the chart below illustrate a continuum of difficulty.

## 1. Simplest

### Mouse in a Hole

A mouse lived in a little hole,

Lived quietly in a little hole.

When all was quiet, as quiet as can be . . .

OUT POPPED HE!

## 2. More Difficult

### *Six Little Ducks*

Six little ducks that I once knew,

Fat ones, skinny ones, fair ones too,

But the one little duck with a feather on his back,

He led the others with his quack-quack-quack.

## 3. Most Difficult

### *Little Nancy Etticoat*

Little Nancy Etticoat

With a white petticoat,

And a red nose;

She has no feet or hands,

The longer she stands,

The shorter she grows.

How I wonder what you are!

Verse 1 is both simple and short. The theme is easy; words are simple with few syllables; there is repetition. Children can say it over and over, substituting other animals. Verse 2 tells a story. The lines are longer and more complex, but the imagery is easy to grasp and the rhythm helps children learn it. Verse 3, "Little Nancy Etticoat," is no longer than "Six Little Ducks," but the theme is more complex and the words more difficult to decode. While the poem has rhythm, it is less pronounced and the rhyme is more subtle. More thinking is demanded of the reader. Of the three selections, only number three has real poetic quality. The others are verses children will enjoy in a way that also helps them to appreciate poetry.

As you select poems to share, consider your children's previous experience, skill with language, and vocabulary. If you begin with easy poems and they learn them very quickly (for example, they join in during shared reading), provide slightly more complex examples.

# Planning for Teaching Opportunities When Revisiting a Text

As short texts, poems provide a multitude of opportunities for learning about language. At first, you will be using the poems only to expand oral language, but the experience will give children plenty of chances to:

- ▶ use interesting language;
- ▶ say and connect words of one, two, and three syllables;
- ▶ say and connect words that rhyme or that begin alike;
- ▶ say words, noticing beginning and ending sounds of consonants; and
- ▶ say words, noticing vowel sounds.

After enjoying a poem several times, you may want to revisit the text with children to help them notice features of print such as letters, letter patterns, or words. The following grid helps you think about the varied opportunities in some sample texts. In each box, we list possible features that children can notice within a poem. You can try planning some poems out for yourself in advance or use the blank grid to keep a record of your teaching points within each poem as you make them.

## WORD-ANALYSIS TEACHING OPPORTUNITIES WHEN REVISITING POETRY

| Title | Type of Text (e.g., limerick, tongue twister, couplet, free verse) | Phonogram Patterns (e.g., -at, -ig, -ate, -ell, -oon) | Letter-Sound (e.g., beginning or ending consonants, consonant digraphs) | High-Frequency Words | Other (e.g., concept words like colors and numbers; names; plurals; rhyming words; syllables; new vocabulary) |
|---|---|---|---|---|---|
| The Little Plant | 3-verse poem Lines 1, 2, and 4 of each verse | -eed, -eep, -ay, -ine, -ose, -at, -ide | Beginning t, h, s, b, d, l, p, f, w, cr, v, r, wh, m  Ending n, t, f, d, p, r, s, l | of, so, light, be | multisyllable words (wonderful), compound words (asleep, sunshine, raindrops, outside) |
| How Much Dew? | tongue twister rhythmic, alliterative poem | -ow, -ew, -op, -ey, -at, -en | Beginning h, m, d, th, wh, dr  Ending w, ch, s, p, f, w, y, t, n | how, much, does, if, they, that, when | one- and two-syllable words, assonance (/o͞o/), plurals with s, compound word (dewdrop) |
| Little Robin Redbreast | 4-line poem with alternate line rhymes | -in, -at, -on | Beginning l, r, s, n, w, h, t  Ending n, st, t, n, l, nt, s, d | sat, went, his, head, tail | one- and two-syllable words, assonance, compound words (redbreast) |
| If You're Happy and You Know It | song with repetition | -ow, -ap, -en, -ace, -ill | Beginning y, h, cl, th, f, w, s, sh  Ending f, y, nd, w, t, p, r, s, n, l | if, happy, know, hand, then, your, show | one- and two-syllable words, contraction (you're) |
| Bat, Bat | 5-line verse with 2 rhyming pairs of lines | -at, -ive, -ice, -on, -en, -ake, -ot | Beginning b, c, m, h, g, y, s, wh, n  Ending t, r, y, d, ll, n, m | under, hat, give, when, if, am | contraction (I'll) multisyllable words (bacon, mistaken) |

# WORD-ANALYSIS TEACHING OPPORTUNITIES WHEN REVISITING POETRY

| Title | Type of Text (e.g., limerick, tongue twister, couplet, free verse) | Phonogram Patterns (e.g., *-at, -ig, -ate, -ell, -oon*) | Letter-Sound (e.g., beginning or ending consonants, consonant digraphs) | High-Frequency Words | Other (e.g., concept words like colors and numbers; names; plurals; rhyming words; syllables; new vocabulary) |
|---|---|---|---|---|---|
| | | | | | |
| | | | | | |
| | | | | | |
| | | | | | |
| | | | | | |

May be photocopied for classroom use. ©2018 by Irene C. Fountas and Gay Su Pinnell from *Sing a Song of Poetry, Grade 1*. Portsmouth, NH: Heinemann.

# Tools for Using Poetry

The tools for working with poetry are simple. You will want to have them well organized and readily available for quick lessons. We suggest the following:

## Easel

A vertical surface for displaying chart paper, or the pocket chart, that is large enough for all children to see and sturdy enough to avoid tipping

## Pocket Chart

A stiff piece of cardboard or plastic that has lines with grooves into which cards can be inserted so that children can work with lines of poems and/ or individual words

## Masks

Cutout cardboard shapes designed to outline words on charts for children to use in locating words or parts of words (see templates in *Teacher Tools*)

## Highlighter Tape

Transparent stick-on tape that can be used to emphasize words, letters, or word parts

## Sticky Notes

Small pieces of paper that have a sticky backing and can temporarily be used to conceal words or parts of words so that children can attend to them

## Flags

A handle with a flat piece of wood or cardboard on the end that can be placed under a word on a chart as a way to locate or emphasize it (see template in *Teacher Tools*)

## Tags

Signs with concise directions so that children can remember an independent work activity; for example, *Read, Mix, Fix, Read* represents *Read* the poem, *Mix* up the sentence strips of a poem, *Fix* the poem back together, and *Read* it again to check it

## Art Materials

Media such as paint, glue, colored paper, and tissue paper

# Instructional Contexts for Poetry

Poetry fits well into the range of activities typical in first-grade classrooms.

## Interactive Read-Aloud

Reading aloud forms a foundation for language and literacy development, and much poetry is meant to be read orally. In addition, reading aloud provides a model of fluent, phrased reading. There are many wonderful picture books that present rhyming verse to children in a very engaging way. For example, the *Fountas & Pinnell Classroom Interactive Read-Aloud Collection, Grade 1* (2018) includes rhyming books like *Mrs. McNosh Hangs Up Her Wash* (Weeks 1988), *Sitting Down to Eat* (Harley 1996), *The Day the Goose Got Loose* (Lindbergh 1990), *One of Each* (Hoberman 1997), and *The Giant Jam Sandwich* (Lord and Burroway 2000).

We recommend repeated readings of favorite poems or rhyming books; it takes many repetitions for children to be able to join in. Ask them to listen the first two or three times you read a verse, but encourage them to join in after they have grasped enough to say it with you, especially on a refrain. In this way, children will begin to internalize much of the language, enjoy it more, and also get the feeling of participating in fluent, phrased reading.

## Shared Reading

Shared reading allows children to both hear the verse and see the print. It uses an enlarged text—a big book or a chart that you have prepared or purchased. Such a shared approach allows you to demonstrate pointing while reading. After one or two repetitions, encourage children to read with you in interactive read-aloud. Be sure that all children can see the visual display of print. You'll want to sit or stand to the side and use a thin pointer (pointers that have objects like balls or hands on the end usually block children's view of the very word you are pointing out). The idea is to maximize children's attention to the print. Shared reading helps them learn how the eyes work in reading. They'll also learn more about rhyme and rhythm.

## Choral Reading and Performance

Choral reading is a more sophisticated version of shared reading. Participants may read from an enlarged text, but often they have their own individual copies. They may have a leader, but it is not always necessary for the leader to point to the words. Participants can practice reading together several times and then perform the piece. You can assign solo lines, boys' and girls' lines, question and response lines, or whole-group lines. If there is dialogue, you can assign roles.

Emphasize varying the voice to suit the meaning of the poem. You can add sound effects (wooden sticks, bells, or other simple tools) or simply invite children to clap or snap their fingers to accentuate words or phrases. Children also love using hand motions.

## Independent Reading

Children love reading poetry, searching for favorite poems, and illustrating poems. A personal poetry book or anthology becomes a treasure. After poems have been read in shared reading, you can reproduce them on smaller pieces of paper. Children glue the poems into a composition book or spiral notebook and illustrate them. Be sure that you are using poems that they are familiar with and can read. Reading their personal poetry books is a good independent reading activity. You can increase the complexity of poems for firstgraders.

## Writing Poetry

Children can begin to get a feel for writing verse through interactive writing. In interactive writing, you and the children compose a message together. You act as a scribe, using the easel, but occasionally children come up and write in a word or letter when you want to draw attention to it. See *Interactive Writing: How Language and Literacy Come Together, K–2* (McCarrier, Pinnell, and Fountas 2000).

You can substitute children's names in a verse or create a variation of one of their favorites (for example, for "Mary Wore Her Red Dress," substitute with different colors or objects). This activity gives them power over language and may inspire children to experiment on their own.

# Types of Poetry

Poetry can be categorized in many different ways: e.g., by pattern, structure, or topic. This book includes rhymes and poems under the headings discussed below, which are related to forms, literary features, and themes. Many of the poems could be placed in more than one category.

## Nursery Rhymes

Traditional rhymes by anonymous poets have been passed down over generations. There are often many different versions. Originally serving as political satire for adults, they have been loved by children for generations. They usually rhyme in couplets or alternating lines and are highly rhythmic. Young children enjoy these simple verses, and nursery rhymes help to build a foundation that will later lead them to a more sophisticated appreciation of poetry. The Mother Goose nursery rhymes, which were published in the eighteenth century, are the best known, but equivalents exist around the world. An example of a Mother Goose nursery rhyme that children love is "Mary Had a Little Lamb":

> Mary had a little lamb,
>
> Little lamb, little lamb.
>
> Mary had a little lamb,
>
> Its fleece was white as snow.
>
> It followed her to school one day,
>
> School one day, school one day.
>
> It followed her to school one day,
>
> Which was against the rule.
>
> It made the children laugh and play,
>
> Laugh and play, laugh and play.
>
> It made the children laugh and play
>
> To see a lamb at school.

## Rhymed Verse

Many poems for young children have lines that end with words that rhyme. These may be *rhyming couplets* (each pair of lines rhyme), as in the poem "What Do You See?":

> What do you see?
>
> A pig in a tree.
>
> Where's your cat?
>
> Under my hat.
>
> How do you know?
>
> He licked my toe.

Or, every other line may rhyme, as in the poem "One for the Money":

> One for the money,
>
> Two for the show,
>
> Three to get ready,
>
> And four to go.

## Free Verse (Unrhymed)

Many poems evoke sensory images and sometimes have rhythm but do not rhyme. Children will enjoy all the different free-verse adjectives and actions, as in those applied to sand in the poem "The Beach" found in *Sing a Song of Poetry, Kindergarten*:

> White sand,
>
> Sea sand,
>
> Warm sand,
>
> Kicking sand,
>
> Building sand,
>
> Watching sand
>
> As the waves roll in.

"Ladies and Gentlemen" is an example of an intriguing poem that has rhythm but does not rhyme:

> Ladies and gentlemen,
>
> Come to supper—
>
> Hot boiled beans
>
> And very good butter.

## Word Play

Some poems like "What's Your Name?" play with words by juxtaposing interesting word patterns in a humorous and playful way:

> What's your name?
>
> Puddin Tame.
>
> Ask me again
>
> And I'll tell you the same.
>
> Where do you live?
>
> In a sieve.
>
> What's your number?
>
> Cucumber!

In word play, we also include *tongue twisters* (poems that are challenging to recite because they play with words that are difficult to pronounce in succession). A well-known example is the poem "Peter Piper":

Peter Piper picked a peck of pickled peppers;

A peck of pickled peppers Peter Piper picked.

If Peter Piper picked a peck of pickled peppers,

Where's the peck of pickled peppers Peter Piper picked?

## Humorous Verse

Humorous verse draws children's attention to absurdities as well as to the sounds and rhythms of language. Sometimes these humorous verses tell nonsense stories. A good example is the poem "There Was an Old Man of Peru" by Edward Lear:

There was an old man of Peru

Who dreamed he was eating his shoe.

He woke in the night

In a terrible fright,

And found it was perfectly true.

## Songs

Songs are musical texts originally intended to be sung. An example is the poem "I Love the Mountains":

I love the mountains.

I love the rolling hills.

I love the flowers.

I love the daffodils.

I love the fireside

When all the lights are low.

Boom-de-otta, boom-de-otta,

Boom-de-otta, boom-de-otta.

You may know the traditional tunes to the songs we have included in this volume. If you don't, compose your own or simply have children chant them while enjoying the rhythm and rhyme.

## Action Songs and Poems

Action poems involve action along with rhythm and rhyme. An example is the poem "I'm a Little Teapot":

> I'm a little teapot,
>
> Short and stout,
>
> Here is my handle,
>
> Here is my spout.
>
> When I get all steamed up,
>
> Hear me shout,
>
> "Tip me over
>
> And pour me out!"

This category also includes *jump-rope songs*, traditional rhymes that children originally chanted while they jumped rope. An example is the poem "Ball-bouncing Rhymes":

> Number one, touch your tongue.
>
> Number two, touch your shoe.
>
> Number three, touch your knee.
>
> Number four, touch the floor.
>
> Number five, dance and jive.
>
> Number six, pick up sticks.
>
> Number seven, say eleven.
>
> Number eight, shut the gate.
>
> Number nine, touch your spine.
>
> Number ten, do it all again!

Children can chant and act out jump-rope songs. There are also chants that accompany games or are simply enjoyable to say together. Chants, like songs, showcase rhythm and rhyme; they are meant to be spoken in chorus rather than set to music. "Counting Polar Bears," for example, is a fast-moving question-and-answer chant:

"Hello, hello, hello, sir.

Meet me at the grocer."

"No, sir."

"Why, sir?"

"Because I have a cold, sir."

"Where did you get your cold, sir?"

"At the North Pole, sir."

"What were you doing there, sir?"

"Counting polar bears, sir."

"How many did you count, sir?"

"One, sir; two, sir; three, sir; four, sir;

Five, sir; six, sir; seven, sir; eight, sir;

Nine, sir; ten, sir."

"Good-bye, good-bye, good-bye, sir!

See you next July, sir."

## Concept Poems

Poems in this category focus on concepts such as numbers, days of the week, colors, ordinal words, seasons, and any other category of information. An example is the poem "Traffic Safety":

Red light says stop.

Green light says go.

Yellow says be careful.

You'd better go slow.

When I reach a crossing place,

To left and right I turn my face.

And then I walk, not run, across the street,

And use my head to guide my feet.

These verses are not only engaging but also easy to learn. As children learn them, they will be repeating the vocabulary that surrounds important concepts.

In the category of concept poems, we also include name poems, which really transcend categories. Many verses present a wonderful opportunity to substitute children's names for names or words already there. In the poem "Papa's Glasses," substitute different children's names for *Papa*. Other poems, like "A Birthday Song" or "Going to the Fair," have blank lines for children to fill in their names.

Many of the poems in the book also offer similar innovations, so look for opportunities. Children will love substituting their own words and phrases. They will develop ownership for the writing and, in the process, become more sensitive to rhymes, syllables, and word patterns.

## Fifty Ways to Use Poems—Plus!

Below we suggest fifty specific ways to use the poems in this volume. Plus, you will notice that each poem includes an instructional suggestion: an easy way to refine and extend the learning and enjoyment potential of each poem. You will find many more ways to engage children in joyful play with oral and written language. The rich collection of poems in this volume can be reproduced, analyzed, or simply read aloud. Enjoy!

Decisions about using poetry depend on your purposes for instruction and the age of the children. By going over favorites again and again, children will internalize rhymes and develop awareness of new language structures. They will become more sensitive to the sounds of language and take pleasure in it. Try out the following suggestions as appropriate to first grade:

1. **Marching to rhymes** Marching around the room while chanting a poem will help children feel the rhythm.

2. **Puppet show** Have children make stick, finger, or sock puppets of their favorite characters in poems and act out the poem as their friends read it. Alternatively, have the puppet say the poem.

3. **Storyboards** Have children draw or paint a backdrop that represents the scene from a rhyme or song. Then have them make cutout figures and glue them on popsicle sticks so that they can move the puppets around in front of the backdrop.

4. **Listening for rhymes** Have children clap or snap their fingers when they come to a rhyming word. They can also say the rhyming word softer (or louder) or mouth the word without making a sound.

5. **Responding** Divide the class in half. Taking a familiar poem, have half the group read (or say) the poem up to the rhyming word and then stop. Let the other half of the class shout the rhyming word.

6. **Recorded poems** Record specific poems on a device so that children can listen independently at a listening center. Include card stock copies of the poems, and show children how to follow along with the recordings.

7. **Class poetry recording** As children learn poems, gradually add to a class recording of their poetry reading or chanting. Keep a table of contents for the audio on a chart and/or place the taped poems in a book. Children can listen to the audio while following along in the book.

8. **Poem pictures** After reading a poem aloud at different times of the day, have children make pictures to go with it and display them with the poem. Duplicate individual copies of a simple poem, and ask each child to illustrate it.

9. **Word endings** Write the poem in large print on a chart or on strips for a pocket chart. After many readings of a poem on a large chart, help children notice words that rhyme and specific vocabulary. They can use a masking card or highlighter tape to mark these words.

10. **Poem innovations** Engage children in noticing and using the language syntax in the poem to create their own similar versions. For example, insert different names in the poem "Jack, Be Nimble" or different foods in the poem "I Like Chocolate."

11. **Personal poetry books** Have children make their own personal poetry books by gluing the poems they experienced in shared reading into spiral notebooks and then illustrating them. Over time they will have a large personal collection of poems to take home.

12. **Little poem books** Make individual poem books, with one line of a poem on each page (for example, "One, Two, Three, Four, Five"). Children can illustrate each page, read the book, and take it home.

13. **Poem performances** Children can perform the poems after they learn them by sometimes adding sound effects with rhythm instruments such as sticks and drums or by clapping and snapping their fingers.

14. **Responsive reading** Find poems such as "Little Pup, Little Pup" that lend themselves to recitation by two or more speakers. Groups of children read questions and answers or alternate lines.

15. **Poetry play** Lead children in saying their favorite poems while they line up, as they walk through an area in which their talking will not disturb other classes, or any time they have a moment of wait time.

16. **Line-up poems** When passing out of the room for recess or lunch, play games in which children say or finish a line of a poem in order to take their place in line.

17. **Rhyming cloze** Read poems, asking children to join in only on the rhyming words. Put highlighter tape on the rhyming words.

18. **Finger poems and action poems** Make finger plays from poems. Act out poems with motions involving the entire body. We have included finger play and action directions for many poems, but you can make up many more.

19. **Poem posters** Use art materials (colored and/or textured paper, pens, crayons, paints) to illustrate poems on charts for the whole group to enjoy or for children to enjoy individually in their personal poetry books.

20. **Poems with blanks** Give children individual copies of poems with a blank space in which they can write their names (or you can write it for them).

21. **Mystery words** In shared reading of a familiar poem, leave out key words but show the first letter so that children can check their reading. You can also use sticky notes and then uncover the word to check it.

22. **Poem displays** Display a poem in several places in the room; children find the poem and use chopstick pointers to read it in small and large versions.

23. **Poetry box** Make a poetry box that contains slightly enlarged and illustrated versions of familiar poems; children can take them out and read them to a classmate.

24. **Poetry board** Make a theme poetry board using poems that explore a concept (for example, animals or vegetables).

25. **Tongue twisters** Make up tongue twisters using the names of children in the class and have them illustrate the verses; for example, Carol carries cookies, carrots, candy, and cucumbers in a cart.

26. **Pocket chart** Place poems on sentence strips in a pocket chart for a variety of activities: substituting words to innovate on the text; highlighting words, letters, or parts of words with colored highlighter tape; putting sentence strips in order for reading; and masking words to make predictions.

27. **Poem puzzles** Have children cut a poem into strips, mix them up, order them, and glue them on paper in the correct order. Then have them use art materials to illustrate the text. Create a simple strip template to photocopy for many different poems.

28. **Class poem or song books** Take one simple, familiar poem and put each line on one page of an oversized class book. Staple the book together. Children can illustrate it and read it to others.

29. **Sequencing poems** Once they have internalized a poem, kindergarteners can write one line of a simple poem on separate pages, staple the pages together as a book, illustrate the pages, and then read their books to others.

30. **More songs and poems** Be on the alert for popular songs that children like or street rhymes that they know. Take appropriate verses from these songs and add them to the poetry collection.

31. **Poem plays** Create a play from the poem. Read the poem (children may join in) while several children act it out.

32. **Poetry dress-up** Collect some simple dress-up items related to the rhymes and poems in your collection. Invite children to dress up for the poem reading.

33. **Poetry party** Have a party to which everyone comes dressed as a character from a poem (props may be made of paper). The group has to guess which poem is represented and then read the poem to the child representing that character.

34. **Character bulletin board** Each child draws a favorite character from a poem and then cuts the figure out. Use interactive writing to create labels for each character on the board.

35. **Poem mashup** Take two favorite poetry characters and have them "meet" each others' poems by including or switching their names.

36. **Favorite poetry recording** Prepare a poetry recording of the children's favorite poems, paper copies of which you can place in a box. Ask the principal, librarian, parents, and other teachers to contribute to the recordings. Children will enjoy listening to the different voices and following the words.

37. **Poetry picnic** Many poems have something to do with food: e.g., "Oats, Peas, Beans." After children have learned a lot of verses, make a list of foods. Consider bringing in samples of the food your class listed. Then children can read or say the poem while eating the food. Be sure to check with families for food allergies and get permission.

38. **Poetry pairs** Children find two poems that go together in some way. They bring the two poems to sharing time and tell how they are alike. You can make a class book of poem pairs with (illustrated) connected poems on opposite pages.

39. **Poetry landscape mural** Children paint a background on which they can glue different landscape mural poetry characters. This mural requires some planning. For example, you would need to draw a mountain for the bear to go over in the poem "The Bear Went over the Mountain."

40. **Poetry sort** Have a box of poems on cards that children know very well and can read. They can read the poems and sort them in any way they want to: e.g., theme (happy, silly, sad), topic (mice, girls, boys, bears), and the way they rhyme (two lines, every other line, no rhyme).

41. **Poems in shapes** Have children read a poem and then glue the poem on a shape (give them a template) that represents it. For example, the poem "Tick-Tock" could be placed on or near a wall clock.

42. **Mixed-up poem** Place a familiar poem on sentence strips in the pocket chart. Mix it up and have children help you rebuild it by saying the lines and looking for the next one. You can also have a correct model displayed beside the cut-up version so that they can check it. Soon children will be able to perform this action on their own.

43. **Picture words** Have children draw pictures for key words in a poem and display them right above the word on a chart.

44. **Hunting for words** Using flyswatters with rectangular holes in the center (or masking cards), have children hunt for particular words or words that rhyme with or start like another.

45. **Word location** Display a familiar poem in the pocket chart, but leave some blanks. Give children the missing key words. Stop when you come to the key word, and ask who has it. Children will need to think about beginning sounds and letters when finding where they go.

46. **Word match** Place one line of a poem in the pocket chart, and have children rebuild the line by matching individual words under the line.

47. **Builder poem** Give each child in a group one word from a poem, written in large print on a card. Have the rest of the class line up these children so that the word order is correct. Then have children take turns walking down the line and saying the poem by pointing to each child and his or her word. Alternatively, have children place the cards in a pocket chart one at a time. They will have to notice when their assigned words come next.

48. **Looking at high-frequency words** The words children encounter over and over in poems will form a core of words that they know and can recognize rapidly. You can have children locate the words to draw attention to them. They can also match word cards by placing like words on top of the words in the poem. An interesting exercise is to create high-frequency words in different fonts. Be sure the words are clear and recognizable. Matching these words to words on a chart or in the pocket chart creates an additional challenge in looking at the features of letters.

49. **Poetry newsletter** Send home a monthly newsletter that tells parents the poems children have learned and provides some poems they can sing or say at home.

50. **Class poetry book** Collect favorite poems into a class book that is small enough to be portable. Children take turns bringing the book home. They can read the poems to friends or family members.

# Poetry Links to Phonics Lessons

In *Fountas & Pinnell Phonics, Spelling, and Word Study Lessons, Grade 1* under Connect Learning Across Contexts, you will find Shared Reading recommendations that enable you to connect learning across the contexts shown in A Design for Responsive Literacy Teaching. Often, the recommendations suggest you turn to *Sing a Song of Poetry* for instructional follow-up using particular poems, songs, and verse. This list links many phonics lessons to a specific poem that extends and refines the instructional aim of the lesson; however, you will notice that not all lessons are linked to a poem, and sometimes, a lesson is linked to two or more poems. What does this mean? The links are completely flexible! Feel free to find and make your own links, and do not feel compelled to use every poem we recommend.

The primary goal of this collection is, quite literally, to sing a song of poetry! Invite children to chant, recite, echo, and play with the poems. Above all, *Sing a Song of Poetry* is meant to inspire a love of language.

## Early Literacy Concepts

**ELC 1**   What Do You See?; The Donkey; One, Two, Three, Four, Five

**ELC 2**   The Elephant Who Jumped a Fence; I Never Had a Dog that Could Talk

**ELC 3**   Little Boy Blue; Did You Feed My Cow?; Soda Bread

**ELC 4**   Bears Eat Honey; Roosters Crow

## Phonological Awareness

| | |
|---|---|
| **PA 1** | Engine, Engine, Number Nine; The Clever Hen; Jack-in-the-box; Ball-bouncing Rhymes |
| **PA 2** | Jack, Be Nimble; A Wise Old Owl; Willy Boy, Willy Boy |
| **PA 3** | Dingle Dangle Scarecrow; Five Fat Peas; Horsie, Horsie |
| **PA 4** | The Queen of Hearts; Little Sally Waters; The Lady with the Alligator Purse |
| **PA 5** | Sing, Sing; A Snail |
| **PA 6** | Little Robin Redbreast; Wiggly Woo |
| **PA 7** | Moon, Moon; I Never Had a Dog that Could Talk; Say and Touch |
| **PA 8** | A Snail; I Never Had a Dog that Could Talk; My Aunt Jane |
| **PA 9** | This Old Man; Tom, Tom, the Piper's Son; On Top of Spaghetti |
| **PA 10** | I Have Two Eyes; Little Blue Ben; Chitterabob |
| **PA 11** | Mary's Canary; Five Little Leaves; Hanky Panky |

## Letter Knowledge

| | |
|---|---|
| **LK 1** | Five Fat Peas; Slowly, Slowly; The Moon Shines Bright |
| **LK 2** | The Little Plant; Merrily We Roll Along; I've Got a Dog as Thin as a Rail |
| **LK 3** | All by Myself; Three Jolly Gentlemen; Nut Tree |
| **LK 4** | Slowly, Slowly; Ladies and Gentlemen; Five Little Sparrows |
| **LK 5** | The Old Gray Cat; My Love for You; Moon, Moon |
| **LK 6** | Up in the Green Orchard; Monday Morning; Out |
| **LK 7** | Out; Mouse in a Hole; Ten Fat Sausages |
| **LK 8** | Handy Pandy; Bumblebee; Good Morning Song |
| **LK 9** | Little Peter Rabbit; Jack, Be Nimble; Mary Wore Her Red Dress |
| **LK 10** | Tom, Tom, the Piper's Son; Polly, Put the Kettle On; Mary Wore Her Red Dress |
| **LK 11** | Bears Eat Honey; 1, 2, 3; Aunt Maria |
| **LK 12** | A Wise Old Owl; A Bicycle Built for Two; The Grand Old Duke of York |
| **LK 13** | Hickory, Dickory, Dean; Slip on Your Raincoat; Three Elephants |
| **LK 14** | Apples and Bananas; Where, Oh, Where Has My Little Dog Gone?; What Do You See? |
| **LK 15** | My Favorite Toys; The Vowel Song; A Snail |

## Letter-Sound Relationships

| | |
|---|---|
| **LSR 1** | Five Little Mice; Bears Eat Honey; Bat, Bat |
| **LSR 2** | It's Raining |
| **LSR 3** | Moon, Moon; Jack, Be Nimble; Johnny Appleseed |
| **LSR 4** | Tick-Tock; The Boy in the Barn; The Elephant Who Jumped a Fence |

## Spelling Patterns

## High-Frequency Words

**HFW 5**  Bears Eat Honey; Roosters Crow; Coffee and Tea

**HFW 6**  A Wise Old Owl; My Aunt Jane; I Have Two Eyes

**HFW 7**  My Big Balloon; My Bike

**HFW 8**  Twenty White Horses; On Saturday Night; Papa's Glasses

## Word Meaning/Vocabulary

**WMV 1**  On Saturday Night; Monday Morning; There Are Seven Days

**WMV 2**  My Favorite Toys; Apples and Bananas; Cap, Mittens, Shoes, and Socks

**WMV 3**  Traffic Safety; A Tiny Seed; My Big Balloon

## Word Structure

**WS 1**  Little Raindrops; Snowman; Two Cats of Kilkenny

**WS 2**  Papa's Glasses; My Favorite Toys; The Smile Song

**WS 3**  It's Raining; The Smile Song

**WS 4**  Crocodile; Shoo Fly; I Would If I Could

**WS 5**  Apples and Bananas; Baby Rhinoceros; Baby Bumblebee; The Grand Old Duke of York

**WS 6**  The Squirrel; What's Your Name?; There's a Hole in the Middle of the Sea

**WS 7**  My Little Toys; I Love the Mountains; Six Little Ducks

**WS 8**  Slip on Your Raincoat; Papa's Glasses; Five Little Sparrows

**WS 9**  This Old Man; Five Little Leaves; Five Enormous Dinosaurs

**WS 10**  The Elephant Who Jumped a Fence; On Top of Spaghetti

## Word-Solving Actions

**WSA 1**  The Elephant Who Jumped a Fence

**WSA 2**  The Smile Song; Six Little Snowmen; A Cloud

**WSA 3**  Star Light, Star Bright; The Little Plant; Little Bird

**WSA 4**  Four Seasons; Aunt Maria; Chitterabob; Good Morning, Mrs. Hen

**WSA 5**  The Little Plant; The Old Woman

**WSA 6**  Hickory, Dickory, Dean; Four Seasons

**WSA 7**  Handy Pandy; Jack Sprat

**WSA 8**  Hickory, Dickory, Dare; I Know Something; My Little Toys

**WSA 10**  Five Fat Peas; The Big Black Bug; I Had a Little Brother

**WSA 11**  Dingle Dangle Scarecrow; My Hat, It Has Three Corners

# 1, 2, 3

1, 2, 3

Father caught a flea.

Put him in a teapot,

To drink a cup of tea.

1, 2, 3

May be photocopied for classroom use. ©2018 by Irene C. Fountas and Gay Su Pinnell from *Sing a Song of Poetry, Grade 1*. Portsmouth, NH: Heinemann.

fold here

**SUGGESTION:** This nonsense poem presents a funny situation. Have children read the poem at a fast pace and then talk about how a *flea* could possibly *drink a cup of tea*. After children know the poem, revisit it to look at words with the letters *ea*.

# Alice the Camel

Alice the camel has five humps.

Alice the camel has five humps.

Alice the camel has five humps.

So ride, Alice, ride.

Boom, boom, boom, boom, boom!

May be photocopied for classroom use. ©2018 by Irene C. Fountas and Gay Su Pinnell from *Sing a Song of Poetry, Grade 1*. Portsmouth, NH: Heinemann.

**SUGGESTION:** Children love to perform this countdown song as a group. In the second verse, Alice has four humps and children say *boom* four times. Then Alice has three humps and children say *boom* three times. This pattern continues until the final verse when Alice transforms into a horse. As they say the three lines about how many humps the camel has, have them bend down at the knees and bounce. As they say the *boom, boom* lines, have them turn to their partner and clap hands together for a high-ten five times, then four, and so forth until there are no camel humps left. When *no humps* is reached, change the last line to: 'Cause Alice is a horse, of course.

# Alice, Where Are You Going?

Alice, where are you going?

Up the stairs to take a bath.

Alice with legs like toothpicks

And a neck like a giraffe.

Alice stepped in the bathtub.

Alice pulled out the plug.

Oh my goodness!

No control!

There goes Alice down that hole.

Alice?

Alice?

Gurgle, gurgle, glug.

May be photocopied for classroom use. ©2018 by Irene C. Fountas and Gay Su Pinnell from *Sing a Song of Poetry, Grade 1*. Portsmouth, NH: Heinemann.

fold here

**SUGGESTION:** This poem may make children think of Alice from Lewis Carroll's *Alice's Adventures in Wonderland* (1865) when she falls down the rabbit hole. If children are not familiar with the story or character, summarize the scene and invite them to identify similarities between it and the poem. Then show the class John Tenniel's illustration of Alice after she eats the small cake that makes her grow big. Invite children to find similarities between the illustration and the poem's descriptions.

# All by Myself

Hat on head, just like this,
Pull it down, you see.
I can put my hat on
All by myself, just me.

One arm in, two arms in,
Buttons, one, two, three.
I can put my coat on
All by myself, just me.

Toes in first, heels down next,
Pull and pull, then see.
I can put my boots on
All by myself, just me.

Fingers here, thumbs right here,
Hands warm as can be.
I can put my mittens on
All by myself, just me.

May be photocopied for classroom use. ©2018 by Irene C. Fountas and Gay Su Pinnell from *Sing a Song of Poetry, Grade 1*. Portsmouth, NH: Heinemann.

fold here

**SUGGESTION:** Invite children to perform this poem as a play. Have a different child act out each verse using actual clothing (or just by pantomiming putting on the garments). Make a shared-writing list of all the things children can do by themselves, and invite them to illustrate it.

# The Ants Go Marching

The ants go marching one by one,

Hurrah, hurrah.

The ants go marching one by one,

Hurrah, hurrah.

The ants go marching one by one,

The little one stops to have some fun.

And they all go marching down,

To the ground,

To get out,

Of the rain.

BOOM! BOOM! BOOM! BOOM!

**ADDITIONAL VERSES:**

two by two . . . tie his shoe

three by three . . . climb a tree

four by four . . . shut the door

five by five . . . take a dive

six by six . . . pick up sticks

seven by seven . . . yell out seven

eight by eight . . . shut the gate

nine by nine . . . check the time

ten by ten . . . say "The End!"

May be photocopied for classroom use. ©2018 by Irene C. Fountas and Gay Su Pinnell from *Sing a Song of Poetry, Grade 1*. Portsmouth, NH: Heinemann.

**SUGGESTION:** Invite children to sing this song to the tune of "When Johnny Comes Marching Home." Show them how to emphasize the word *down* and how to use a mechanical repetitive tone (like a drum) for lines ending with the words *down*, *ground*, and *rain*. Then have children say the last line loudly.

fold here

# Apples and Bananas

I like to eat eat eat apples and bananas.
I like to eat eat eat apples and bananas.

I like to ate ate ate ay-ples and bay-nay-nays.
I like to ate ate ate ay-ples and bay-nay-nays.

I like to eat eat eat ee-ples and bee-nee-nees.
I like to eat eat eat ee-ples and bee-nee-nees.

I like to ite, ite, ite, i-ples and bi-ni-nis.
I like to ite, ite, ite, i-ples and bi-ni-nis.

I like to ote ote ote o-ples and bo-no-nos.
I like to ote ote ote o-ples and bo-no-nos.

I like to ute ute ute u-ples and bu-nu-nus.
I like to ute ute ute u-ples and bu-nu-nus.

Now we're through, through, through, through,
Now we're through with the apples and bananas,
Now we're through, through, through, through,
With a, e, i, o, and u.

May be photocopied for classroom use. ©2018 by Irene C. Fountas and Gay Su Pinnell from *Sing a Song of Poetry, Grade 1.* Portsmouth, NH: Heinemann.

fold here

**SUGGESTION:** This is a playful song with a catchy tune. The words change to reflect long vowel sounds. Children will catch on and enjoy making up their own verses featuring other foods.

# Aunt Maria

Aunt Maria, she sat on the fire.

The fire was too hot, she sat on the pot.

The pot was too round, she sat on the ground.

The ground was too flat, she sat on the cat.

The cat ran away with Maria on her back.

May be photocopied for classroom use. ©2018 by Irene C. Fountas and Gay Su Pinnell from *Sing a Song of Poetry, Grade 1*. Portsmouth, NH: Heinemann.

**SUGGESTION:** Invite children to substitute first and last names of classmates. Have them highlight simple phonograms such as /at/ and /ot/.

fold here

# Auntie, Will Your Dog Bite?

Auntie, will your dog bite?

No, child, no!

Chicken in the bread tray,

Making up dough.


Auntie, will your oven bake?

Yes, just try!

What's that chicken good for?

Pie! Pie! Pie!


Auntie, is your pie good?

Good as you can expect!

Chicken in the bread tray,

Peck! Peck! Peck!

May be photocopied for classroom use. ©2018 by Irene C. Fountas and Gay Su Pinnell from *Sing a Song of Poetry, Grade 1*. Portsmouth, NH: Heinemann.

fold here

**SUGGESTION:** Assign individual children to read the questions while the rest of the class recites the answers. You may need to help children differentiate between roles by highlighting their respective lines.

# Autumn Leaves

Autumn leaves are falling, falling, falling.

Autumn leaves are spinning, spinning, spinning.

Autumn leaves are floating, floating, floating.

Autumn leaves are turning, turning, turning.

Autumn leaves are dancing, dancing, dancing.

Autumn leaves are blowing, blowing, blowing.

Autumn leaves are falling, falling, falling.

Autumn leaves are sleeping, sleeping, sleeping.

May be photocopied for classroom use. ©2018 by Irene C. Fountas and Gay Su Pinnell from *Sing a Song of Poetry, Grade 1*. Portsmouth, NH: Heinemann.

fold here

**SUGGESTION:** Children enjoy acting out this poem—especially outside if the autumn leaves really are falling! Invite them to use the predictable pattern *Autumn leaves are* to create their own descriptive lines of poetry and prose: e.g., *Winter snowflakes are, Spring petals are*, or perhaps even *Summer sand is*. Pair this poem with Lois Ehlert's *Red Leaf, Yellow Leaf* (1991). They can also talk about how the repetition makes the poem more effective; for example, they could say it without repeating the last two words in each line and compare the versions.

# Baby Bumblebee

I'm bringing home a baby bumblebee.

Won't my mother be so proud of me?

I'm bringing home a baby bumblebee.

Ouch! He stung me!

**ADDITIONAL VERSES:**

I'm talking to my baby bumblebee.
Won't my mother be so proud of me?
I'm talking to my baby bumblebee.
"Oh," he said, "I'm sorry."

I'm letting go my baby bumblebee.
Won't my mother be so proud of me?
I'm letting go my baby bumblebee.
Look! He's happy to be free!

May be photocopied for classroom use. ©2018 by Irene C. Fountas and Gay Su Pinnell from *Sing a Song of Poetry, Grade 1*. Portsmouth, NH: Heinemann.

fold here

**SUGGESTION:** Invite children to pretend to have a trapped bumblebee while reciting the first verse. Once they are familiar with it, teach children the poem's second and third verses. Have them pantomime talking to their imaginative bumblebee before finally setting it free.

# Baby Rhinoceros

We're bringing home a baby rhinoceros.

Won't our mothers be so proud of us?

'Cause we're bringing home a baby rhinoceros.

Oops! He swallowed us!

May be photocopied for classroom use. ©2018 by Irene C. Fountas and Gay Su Pinnell from *Sing a Song of Poetry, Grade 1.* Portsmouth, NH: Heinemann.

ACTIONS:

We're bringing home a baby rhinoceros. [*place both hands over one shoulder as if dragging something heavy*]

Won't our mothers be so proud of us?

'Cause we're bringing home a baby rhinoceros.

Oops! He swallowed us! [*children fall on the floor*]

SUGGESTION: This adaptation of the "Baby Bumblebee" poem is good for group enactment as indicated in the actions above. If the classroom is crowded, have children scrunch down into a ball on the floor instead of falling. Alternatively, invite the class to brainstorm new adaptations: e.g., *I'm bringing home a joey / Won't my mom be so proud of me? / 'Cause I'm bringing home a joey. / Oops! He bounced away from me!* Children may need you to explain that a *joey* is a baby kangaroo.

fold here

# Ball-bouncing Rhymes

Number one, touch your tongue.

Number two, touch your shoe.

Number three, touch your knee.

Number four, touch the floor.

Number five, dance and jive.

Number six, pick up sticks.

Number seven, say eleven.

Number eight, shut the gate.

Number nine, touch your spine.

Number ten, do it all again!

May be photocopied for classroom use. ©2018 by Irene C. Fountas and Gay Su Pinnell from *Sing a Song of Poetry, Grade 1*. Portsmouth, NH: Heinemann.

**SUGGESTION:** Have the class recite the poem as children bounce a ball and perform the actions. Toss the ball to student number one, who bounces it once and performs the first line's action. This child passes or tosses the ball to student number two, who bounces it twice, performs the second line's action, and then passes the ball to student number three. Have children repeat this pattern through student number ten or until everyone has had a turn.

# Bat, Bat

Bat, bat, come under my hat,

And I'll give you a slice of bacon.

And when I bake,

I'll give you a cake,

If I am not mistaken.

May be photocopied for classroom use. ©2018 by Irene C. Fountas and Gay Su Pinnell from *Sing a Song of Poetry, Grade 1*. Portsmouth, NH: Heinemann.

**SUGGESTION:** This poem has infectious rhymes and humorous imagery. Invite children to substitute other *b* words for *bat*, such as *bird*, *butterfly*, or *bee*.

fold here

# Bears Eat Honey

Bears eat honey.

Cows eat corn.

What do you eat

When you get up in the morn?


Monkeys eat bananas.

Cows eat corn.

What do you eat

When you get up in the morn?


Horses eat oats,

Cows eat corn,

What do you eat

When you get up in the morn?

May be photocopied for classroom use. ©2018 by Irene C. Fountas and Gay Su Pinnell from *Sing a Song of Poetry, Grade 1*. Portsmouth, NH: Heinemann.

fold here

**SUGGESTION:** Use interactive writing to answer each verse: e.g., cereal, pancakes, or oatmeal. Later, invite children to use these items to create more verses.

# Bees

If bees stay at home,

Rain will soon come.

If they fly away,

Fine will be the day.

May be photocopied for classroom use. ©2018 by Irene C. Fountas and Gay Su Pinnell from *Sing a Song of Poetry, Grade 1*. Portsmouth, NH: Heinemann.

**SUGGESTION:** Discuss the idea that bees might fly to gather pollen when the sun is shining brightly. Children may notice that the words *home* and *come* look the same but don't rhyme. Alternatively, they may notice that the words *away* and *day* both look the same and rhyme.

fold here

# A Bicycle Built for Two

Daisy, Daisy, give me your answer true.

I'm half crazy all for the love of you.

It won't be a stylish marriage.

I can't afford a carriage.

But you'll look sweet, upon the seat

Of a bicycle built for two.

May be photocopied for classroom use. ©2018 by Irene C. Fountas and Gay Su Pinnell from *Sing a Song of Poetry, Grade 1*. Portsmouth, NH: Heinemann.

**SUGGESTION:** Children are probably not familiar with this song. Teach it to them and sing it together. A bicycle built for two may be a new concept to them. Before discussing the idea in depth, invite children to draw, dictate, or write about what a bicycle built for two might look like. Share and discuss these ideas; if possible, share a drawing or photograph, an Internet image, or a video of the real thing.

# The Big Black Bug

The big black bug

Bit the big black bear,

But the big black bear

Bit the big black bug back!

May be photocopied for classroom use. ©2018 by Irene C. Fountas and Gay Su Pinnell from *Sing a Song of Poetry, Grade 1.* Portsmouth, NH: Heinemann.

fold here

**SUGGESTION:** Children may not know what a tongue twister is. After explaining, invite them to practice saying the verse slowly at first and then faster with each rereading. Support them by presenting one line at a time and having them repeat the line back to you. You can also display this poem in a pocket chart and substitute words (*brown* for *black*) as the children become faster at reciting.

# A Birthday Song

_____ has a birthday.

We're so glad!

We hope that _____ birthday

Is the best _____ has ever had!

May be photocopied for classroom use. ©2018 by Irene C. Fountas and Gay Su Pinnell from *Sing a Song of Poetry, Grade 1.* Portsmouth, NH: Heinemann.

fold here

**SUGGESTION:** Make this a traditional birthday ritual for each child in the class. Let children with summer birthdays pick a day in April or May. Make the poem on chart paper or in a pocket chart so it can be revisited often. Be sure to point out that the third line changes (*his, her* and *he, she* accordingly).

# The Boy in the Barn

A little boy went into a barn,

And lay down on some hay.

An owl came out and flew about,

And the little boy ran away.

May be photocopied for classroom use. ©2018 by Irene C. Fountas and Gay Su Pinnell from *Sing a Song of Poetry, Grade 1*. Portsmouth, NH: Heinemann.

**SUGGESTION:** Some children may need background on what a barn is and why there might be hay and an owl there. Have them discuss why the boy ran away.

fold here

# Bumblebee

Bumblebee was in the barn,

Carrying dinner under his arm.

Buzzzzzzz-zz-z!

May be photocopied for classroom use. ©2018 by Irene C. Fountas and Gay Su Pinnell from *Sing a Song of Poetry, Grade 1*. Portsmouth, NH: Heinemann.

ACTIONS:

Bumblebee was in the barn, [*circle finger in the air*]

Carrying dinner under his arm. [*move finger close to arm*]

Buzzzzzzz-zz-z! [*poke arm*]

fold here

**SUGGESTION:** Children will enjoy this nonsense poem. You may want to call attention to the word *buzz* and discuss the idea that this word actually sounds like the noise the bee makes.

# Bunch of Blue Ribbons

Oh, dear, what can the matter be?

Oh, dear, what can the matter be?

Oh, dear, what can the matter be?

Johnny's so long at the fair.


He promised to buy me a bunch of blue ribbons,

He promised to buy me a bunch of blue ribbons,

He promised to buy me a bunch of blue ribbons,

To tie up my bonny brown hair.

May be photocopied for classroom use. ©2018 by Irene C. Fountas and Gay Su Pinnell from *Sing a Song of Poetry, Grade 1*. Portsmouth, NH: Heinemann.

**SUGGESTION:** Display this poem in a pocket chart and present a list of different colors on word cards below it. Invite children to substitute the word card for *blue* with word cards for other colors. You may want to explain that *bonny* is another word for *pretty*.

fold here

# Can You Can?

Can you

Can a can

As a canner

Can can

A can?

May be photocopied for classroom use. ©2018 by Irene C. Fountas and Gay Su Pinnell from *Sing a Song of Poetry, Grade 1*. Portsmouth, NH: Heinemann.

fold here

**SUGGESTION:** Have children highlight or underline the word *can*, including part of the word *canner*. Discuss the two meanings of *can*.

# Can You Wash Your Father's Shirt?

Can you wash your father's shirt,

Can you wash it clean?

Can you wash your father's shirt,

And bleach it on the green?


Yes, I can wash my father's shirt,

And I can wash it clean.

I can wash my father's shirt,

And send it to the Queen.

May be photocopied for classroom use. ©2018 by Irene C. Fountas and Gay Su Pinnell from *Sing a Song of Poetry, Grade 1*. Portsmouth, NH: Heinemann.

fold here

**SUGGESTION:** Have half the children read the first verse and the other half read the second. Invite them to imagine what the line *bleach it on the green* might mean. Explain that the word *green* refers to a lawn and that sunshine will remove color or *bleach* something.

# Cap, Mittens, Shoes, and Socks

Cap, mittens, shoes, and socks,

Shoes and socks.

Cap, mittens, shoes, and socks,

Shoes and socks.

And pants and belt, and shirt and tie,

Go together wet or dry,

Wet or dry!

May be photocopied for classroom use. ©2018 by Irene C. Fountas and Gay Su Pinnell from *Sing a Song of Poetry, Grade 1*. Portsmouth, NH: Heinemann.

fold here

**SUGGESTION:** Have children sing to the tune of "Head, Shoulders, Knees, and Toes." After they are familiar with the words, ask a select group to recite only the echoing lines *Shoes and socks* and *Wet or dry!* The rest of the class can choose to recite the poem as it is, or reorder the line *Cap, mittens, shoes, and socks*. Whichever order the group chooses, the second group must echo. While children sing, help them keep the beat by clapping your hands and inviting them to do the same.

# Catalina Magnalina

She has a peculiar name but she wasn't to blame,
She got it from her mother, who's the same, same, same.

*Chorus*

   Catalina Magnalina, Hootensteiner Bogentwiner

   Hogan Logan Bogan was her name.

She had two peculiar teeth in her mouth,
One pointed north and the other pointed south,
south, south.

*Chorus*

She had two peculiar eyes in her head,
One was purple and the other one was red, red, red.

*Chorus*

May be photocopied for classroom use. ©2018 by Irene C. Fountas and Gay Su Pinnell from *Sing a Song of Poetry, Grade 1*. Portsmouth, NH: Heinemann.

SUGGESTION: Sing the song to the tune of "There Was a Crooked Man." You may want to clap the four-syllable words in the chorus. Explain what a *chorus* is (sometimes known as a *refrain*).

fold here

# A Caterpillar Crawled

A caterpillar crawled

To the top of the tree.

"I think I'll take a nap," said he.

So under a leaf he began to creep

To spin his cocoon,

And he fell asleep.


All winter long he slept in his bed,

'Til spring came along one day and said,

"Wake up, wake up, little sleepyhead,

Wake up, it's time to get out of bed."

So he opened his eyes that sunshiny day.

Lo! He was a butterfly and flew away.

May be photocopied for classroom use. ©2018 by Irene C. Fountas and Gay Su Pinnell from *Sing a Song of Poetry, Grade 1*. Portsmouth, NH: Heinemann.

**SUGGESTION:** Invite children to act out *crawl* by having the first two fingers of one hand creep up their other arm as they say the first two lines. Then have them close one hand over the other during the rest of the first verse. For *wake up*, ask children to shake one hand; then have them lock their thumbs and wave the fingers of both hands as the butterfly flies away.

# The Cats Have Come to Tea

*by Kate Greenaway*

What did she see—oh, what did she see,
As she stood leaning against the tree?
Why all the cats had come to tea.

What a fine turnout—from round about,
All the houses had let them out,
And here they were with scamper and shout.

"Mew–mew–mew!" was all they could say,
And, "We hope we find you well today."

Oh, what should she do—oh, what should she do?
What a lot of milk they would get through;
For here they were with, "Mew–mew–mew!"

She didn't know—oh, she didn't know,
If bread and butter they'd like or no;
They might want little mice, oh! oh! oh!

Dear me—oh, dear me,
All the cats had come to tea.

May be photocopied for classroom use. ©2018 by Irene C. Fountas and Gay Su Pinnell from *Sing a Song of Poetry, Grade 1*. Portsmouth, NH: Heinemann.

**SUGGESTION:** This poem is fun to role-play. Invite children to be the cats coming to tea by reciting their respective lines while you narrate the rest of the poem. Children can dress up or make paper tea-time props to help them act out their parts. After they are familiar with the poem, ask the class to think about other animals they could invite to tea, and have them change the poem accordingly—sound effects included!

fold here

# Chitterabob

There was a man,

And his name was Dob.

And he had a wife,

And her name was Mob.

And he had a dog,

And he called it Cob.

And she had a cat,

Called Chitterabob.

"Cob," says Dob.

"Chitterabob," says Mob.

Cob was Dob's dog,

Chitterabob Mob's cat.

May be photocopied for classroom use. ©2018 by Irene C. Fountas and Gay Su Pinnell from *Sing a Song of Poetry, Grade 1*. Portsmouth, NH: Heinemann.

fold here

**SUGGESTION:** Children will love learning and practicing this tongue twister. After they are familiar with the words, try dividing the group in two and ask them to alternate lines as they recite; one group makes a statement and the other responds with the follow-up line.

# The Clever Hen

I had a little hen,

The prettiest ever seen.

She washed the dishes

And kept the house clean.


She went to the mill

To fetch some flour.

She brought it home

In less than an hour.


She baked some bread,

And took in the mail.

She sat by the fire,

And told many a fine tale.

May be photocopied for classroom use. ©2018 by Irene C. Fountas and Gay Su Pinnell from *Sing a Song of Poetry, Grade 1*. Portsmouth, NH: Heinemann.

**SUGGESTION:** After children are familiar with this verse, introduce the talking mother from "Good Morning, Mrs. Hen" (also in this volume). Then pair this rhyme with the classic folktale *The Little Red Hen* by Lucinda McQueen (1985) or the alternative adaptation *The Little Red Hen: An Old Fable* by Heather Forest (2006)—both found in the *Fountas & Pinnell Classroom™ Interactive Read-Aloud Collection, Grade 1* (2018).

fold here

# The Clock

There's a neat little clock,

In the schoolroom it stands,

And it points to the time

With its two little hands.


And may we, like the clock,

Keep a face clean and bright,

With hands ever ready

To do what is right.

May be photocopied for classroom use. ©2018 by Irene C. Fountas and Gay Su Pinnell from *Sing a Song of Poetry, Grade 1*. Portsmouth, NH: Heinemann.

fold here

**SUGGESTION:** After children know the poem, you may want to talk about the comparisons in it: e.g., a person's face and hands with the clock's face and hands.

# A Cloud

What's fluffy white and floats up high,

Like a pile of cotton in the sky?

And when the wind blows hard and strong,

What very gently floats along?

What brings the rain, what brings the snow,

That showers down on us below?

When you look up in the high blue sky,

What is that thing you see float by?

A cloud!

ACTIONS:

What's fluffy white and floats up high, [*point skyward*]

Like a pile of cotton in the sky?

And when the wind blows hard and strong, [*wiggle fingers moving horizontally*]

What very gently floats along?

What brings the rain, what brings the snow, [*open hands palm up*]

That showers down on us below? [*wiggle fingers moving downward*]

When you look up in the high blue sky, [*look up*]

What is that thing you see float by?

A cloud!

SUGGESTION: Present this poem as a riddle (without the title and last line), and ask children to predict the answer. Invite them to think of other things (besides cotton) that clouds remind them of, or help them make a web of words related to clouds (drawing from the poem).

May be photocopied for classroom use. ©2018 by Irene C. Fountas and Gay Su Pinnell from *Sing a Song of Poetry, Grade 1*. Portsmouth, NH: Heinemann.

fold here

# Cock-a-doodle-doo!

Cock-a-doodle-doo!

My dame has lost her shoe.

My master's lost his fiddling stick,

And doesn't know what to do.


Cock-a-doodle-doo!

What is my dame to do?

Till master finds his fiddling stick,

She'll dance without her shoe.

May be photocopied for classroom use. ©2018 by Irene C. Fountas and Gay Su Pinnell from *Sing a Song of Poetry, Grade 1.* Portsmouth, NH: Heinemann.

fold here

**SUGGESTION:** Create some rhythmical sound to accompany *Cock-a-doodle-doo* by inviting some of the children to tap sticks, shake a tambourine, or ring bells.

# Coffee and Tea

My sister, Molly, and I fell out,

And what do you think it was about?

She loved coffee and I loved tea,

And that was the reason we couldn't agree.

May be photocopied for classroom use. ©2018 by Irene C. Fountas and Gay Su Pinnell from *Sing a Song of Poetry, Grade 1.* Portsmouth, NH: Heinemann.

SUGGESTION: Substitute *My sister, Molly,* for *My friend* _____ on the first line. Explain how *falling out* means "to argue." Have partners substitute other foods for coffee and tea, providing a chance for children to create contrasts. Don't worry too much about preserving the rhyme on the last two lines; children will enjoy manipulating the language.

fold here

# Counting Polar Bears

"Hello, hello, hello, sir.

Meet me at the grocer."

"No, sir."

"Why, sir?"

"Because I have a cold, sir."

"Where did you get your cold, sir?"

"At the North Pole, sir."

"What were you doing there, sir?"

"Counting polar bears, sir."

"How many did you count, sir?"

"One, sir; two, sir; three, sir; four, sir;

Five, sir; six, sir; seven, sir; eight, sir;

Nine, sir; ten, sir."

"Good-bye, good-bye, good-bye, sir!

See you next July, sir."

May be photocopied for classroom use. ©2018 by Irene C. Fountas and Gay Su Pinnell from *Sing a Song of Poetry, Grade 1*. Portsmouth, NH: Heinemann.

fold here

**SUGGESTION:** Children may perform this verse in two groups, or two children may act out the conversing roles. Let the class take the lead and figure it out their way. After some practice, have them say the poem faster and especially pick up the pace when counting.

# Crocodile

If you should meet a crocodile,

Don't take a stick and poke him.

Ignore the welcome of his smile,

Be careful not to stroke him.

For as he sleeps upon the Nile,

He gets thinner and thinner.

Remember when you meet a crocodile,

He's looking for his dinner.

May be photocopied for classroom use. ©2018 by Irene C. Fountas and Gay Su Pinnell from *Sing a Song of Poetry, Grade 1*. Portsmouth, NH: Heinemann.

**SUGGESTION:** Compare this poem with "The Lady and the Crocodile" (also in this volume). You may want to point out on a map that the Nile is a river in Africa.

fold here

# Did You Feed My Cow?

Did you feed my cow?

Yes, ma'am!

Will you tell me how?

Yes, ma'am!

What did you feed her?

Corn and hay.

What did you feed her?

Corn and hay.


Did you milk her good?

Yes, ma'am!

Did you milk her like you should?

Yes, ma'am!

How did you milk her?

Swish, swish, swish!

How did you milk her?

Swish, swish, swish.

May be photocopied for classroom use. ©2018 by Irene C. Fountas and Gay Su Pinnell from *Sing a Song of Poetry, Grade 1*. Portsmouth, NH: Heinemann.

**SUGGESTION:** After children have heard the poem and are familiar with the question-and-answer format, you may want to ask the questions and have children respond in unison with their lines. Invite some of the children to read the questions; have the rest of the class respond. Discuss when it would be appropriate to change *ma'am* to *sir*. Having the poem in a pocket chart can make the substitution easy.

# Dig a Little Hole

*added stanzas by Kate Roth*

Dig a little hole.
Plant a little seed.
Pour a little water.
Pull a little weed.

Chase a little bug.
Oh! There he goes!
Give a little sunshine.
See the little rose!

Dig another hole.
Plant another seed.
Pour some more water.
Pull another weed.

Chase another bug.
Oh! There he goes!
Give some more sunshine.
See another rose!

May be photocopied for classroom use. ©2018 by Irene C. Fountas and Gay Su Pinnell from *Sing a Song of Poetry, Grade 1*. Portsmouth, NH: Heinemann.

**SUGGESTION:** Ask children for their recommendations on adding actions or movements. This poem can also be the basis for a great mural. Put the stanzas on heavy art paper and invite children to make cut- or torn-paper illustrations. Move the pieces around until the group is satisfied with the arrangement before gluing them down. Children can then stand in front of the mural and recite the poem while they perform the appropriate actions.

fold here

# Dingle Dangle Scarecrow

When all the cows were sleeping
And the sun had gone to bed,
Up jumped the scarecrow
And this is what he said:

*Chorus*
"I'm a dingle dangle scarecrow
With a flippy floppy hat!
I can shake my arms like this,
I can shake my legs like that!"

When the cows were in the meadow
And the pigeons in the loft,
Up jumped the scarecrow
And whispered very soft:

*Chorus*

When all the hens were roosting
And the moon behind a cloud,
Up jumped the scarecrow
And shouted very loud:

*Chorus*

May be photocopied for classroom use. ©2018 by Irene C. Fountas and Gay Su Pinnell from *Sing a Song of Poetry, Grade 1*. Portsmouth, NH: Heinemann.

**SUGGESTION:** There's a lot going on in this poem about a scarecrow who waits until farm creatures are sleeping and then scares them! Children will need to hear the poem several times to understand all the things that are happening. This story poem is a great one to stage, with parts for *cows, pigeons, hens,* and one *dingle dangle scarecrow* who comes to life, shakes his arms and legs, and flippy flops his hat. Other animals may be added as well. Remind children that a *chorus*—also called a *refrain*—is "the part you say over and over."

# The Donkey

I saw a donkey

One day old,

His head was too big

For his neck to hold;

His legs were shaky

And long and loose,

They rocked and staggered

And weren't much use.

ADDITIONAL VERSE:

He tried to gambol
And frisk a bit,
But he wasn't quite sure
Of the trick of it.
His queer little coat
Was soft and gray,
And curled at his neck
In a lovely way.

May be photocopied for classroom use. ©2018 by Irene C. Fountas and Gay Su Pinnell from *Sing a Song of Poetry, Grade 1.* Portsmouth, NH: Heinemann.

**SUGGESTION:** This poem evokes an image of a newborn animal. Most children will not have seen a newborn animal but can imagine a tiny donkey with curly fur just learning to walk. They can talk about what the donkey might look like. If you present the second verse, point out that *gambol* and *frisk* both mean: "to skip around playfully."

fold here

# Down on the Farm

*Chorus*

Oh, we're on our way, we're on our way to the farm,

We're on our way, we're on our way to the farm, farm.

Down on the farm there is a big brown cow.

Down on the farm there is a big brown cow.

The cow, she makes a sound like this: Moo! Moo!

The cow, she makes a sound like this: Moo! Moo!

*Chorus*

Down on the farm there is a little red hen.

Down on the farm there is a little red hen.

The hen, she makes a sound like this: Cluck, Cluck!

The hen, she makes a sound like this: Cluck, Cluck!

*Chorus*

May be photocopied for classroom use. ©2018 by Irene C. Fountas and Gay Su Pinnell from *Sing a Song of Poetry, Grade 1*. Portsmouth, NH: Heinemann.

fold here    **SUGGESTION:** Substitute a variety of other animals and the sounds they make such as: *big black dog—Bow-wow! big brown horse—Neigh! Neigh!*

# The Elephant Who Jumped a Fence

I asked my mother for fifty cents

To see an elephant jump a fence.

He jumped so high, he reached the sky,

And didn't get back till the Fourth of July.


I asked my mother for fifty more

To see the elephant scrub the floor.

He scrubbed so slow he stubbed his toe,

And that was the end of the elephant show.

May be photocopied for classroom use. ©2018 by Irene C. Fountas and Gay Su Pinnell from *Sing a Song of Poetry, Grade 1*. Portsmouth, NH: Heinemann.

**SUGGESTION:** Children may perform the poem using a paper fence and an elephant cutout or puppet. It's fun to imagine an elephant flying, and children enjoy attending to the rhyming words in a variety of ways: e.g., clapping, snapping, shouting, or tapping. There are two other elephant rhymes in this volume. After the class has enjoyed the jumping elephant who scrubs floors, introduce them to other elephants in "Way Down South" and "Three Elephants."

# Engine, Engine, Number Nine

Engine, engine, number nine,

Running on Chicago line.

See it sparkle, see it shine.

Engine, engine, number nine.

Toot-toot! Toot-toot!


Engine, engine, number nine,

Running on Chicago line.

If the train should jump the track,

Do you want your money back?

Toot-toot! Toot-toot!

May be photocopied for classroom use. ©2018 by Irene C. Fountas and Gay Su Pinnell from *Sing a Song of Poetry, Grade 1*. Portsmouth, NH: Heinemann.

fold here

**SUGGESTION:** Ask children to substitute any two- or three-syllable city name for *Chicago*. Have them clap the names to see if they will fit. Invite children to sit in a line, locomotive style, and rock forward and backward to the rhythm of the train. Add some instruments—bell, train whistle, and so forth—to go along with *Toot-toot!*

# Five Bananas

Five bananas on a banana tree,

Three for you and two for me.

Five bananas on a banana tree

Oh! I love those bananas!


Four bananas on a banana tree,

Two for you and two for me.

Four bananas on a banana tree

Oh! I love those bananas!

ADDITIONAL VERSES:

Three bananas on a banana tree,
Two for you and one for me.
Three bananas on a banana tree
Oh! I love those bananas!

Two bananas on a banana tree,
One for you and one for me.
Two bananas on a banana tree
Oh! I love those bananas!

One banana on a banana tree,
Half for you and half for me.
One banana on a banana tree
Oh! I love those bananas!

No bananas on the banana tree,
None for you and none for me.
No bananas on the banana tree
Oh! We have no bananas!

May be photocopied for classroom use. ©2018 by Irene C. Fountas and Gay Su Pinnell from *Sing a Song of Poetry, Grade 1*. Portsmouth, NH: Heinemann.

**SUGGESTION:** This is a good poem to use in a pocket chart. Substitute the number words in each stanza, and practice addition and subtraction equations using bananas and other fruit; children can write the equations on the board. Invite your class to hold up the right number of fingers as they say each number word. Other visuals may be used, such as a feltboard with cutout bananas or a whiteboard with banana cutouts held on with two-sided tape.

fold here

# Five Enormous Dinosaurs

Five enormous dinosaurs,
Letting out a roar—
One went away, and
Then there were four.

Four enormous dinosaurs,
Crashing down a tree—
One went away, and
Then there were three.

Three enormous dinosaurs,
Eating tiger stew—
One went away, and
Then there were two.

Two enormous dinosaurs,
Trying hard to run—
One went away, and
Then there was one.

One enormous dinosaur,
Afraid to be a hero—
He went away, and
Then there was zero.

May be photocopied for classroom use. ©2018 by Irene C. Fountas and Gay Su Pinnell from *Sing a Song of Poetry, Grade 1*. Portsmouth, NH: Heinemann.

fold here

**SUGGESTION:** Divide the class into five groups and invite each to make an *enormous dinosaur* puppet using craft materials found in the classroom. Then ask each group to hold up its dinosaur puppet while the class recites the poem. At the end of the first stanza, group one and its dinosaur puppet sit down. Then, on cue, each group thereafter sits until there's only one *enormous dinosaur* left who is *afraid to be a hero*.

# Five Fat Peas

Five fat peas in a pea pod pressed,

One grew, two grew, and so did the rest.

They grew and grew and did not stop,

Until one day the pod went POP!

May be photocopied for classroom use. ©2018 by Irene C. Fountas and Gay Su Pinnell from *Sing a Song of Poetry, Grade 1*. Portsmouth, NH: Heinemann.

**SUGGESTION:** Children love the images this infectious counting rhyme conjures: peas growing and the pea pod popping. Invite your class to clap when the pod goes *POP!*

fold here

# Five Little Chickadees

Five little chickadees peeping at the door,

One flew away and then there were four;

Chickadee, chickadee, happy and gay,

Chickadee, chickadee, fly away.

ADDITONAL VERSES:

Four little chickadees sitting on a tree . . .

Three little chickadees looking at you . . .

Two little chickadees sitting in the sun . . .

One little chickadee sitting there as one,

It flew away and then there was none . . .

May be photocopied for classroom use. ©2018 by Irene C. Fountas and Gay Su Pinnell from *Sing a Song of Poetry, Grade 1*. Portsmouth, NH: Heinemann.

fold here

**SUGGESTION:** Invite five children to stand in front of the whole class and *fly away* one by one as the verses are recited.

# Five Little Firefighters

Five little firefighters standing in a row;
One, two, three, four, five, they go.
Hop on the engine with a shout,
Quicker than a wink the fire is out!

Four little firefighters standing in a row;
One, two, three, four, whoosh! they go.
Hop on the engine with a shout,
Quicker than a wink the fire is out!

Three little firefighters standing in a row;
One, two, three, whoosh! whoosh! they go.
Hop on the engine with a shout,
Quicker than a wink the fire is out!

ADDITIONAL VERSES:

Two little firefighters standing in a row;
One, two, whoosh! whoosh! whoosh! they go.
Hop on the engine with a shout,
Quicker than a wink the fire is out!

One little firefighter standing in a row;
One, whoosh! whoosh! whoosh! whoosh! she goes.
Hop on the engine with a shout,
Quicker than a wink the fire is out!
No little firefighters standing in a row;
Whoosh! whoosh! whoosh! whoosh! whoosh!

May be photocopied for classroom use. ©2018 by Irene C. Fountas and Gay Su Pinnell from *Sing a Song of Poetry, Grade 1.* Portsmouth, NH: Heinemann.

**SUGGESTION:** Use this verse as a finger play or ask children to act out the poem. Invite them to make the engine by placing five chairs in formation. Children will love to be one of the firefighters hopping on board the fire truck and then dropping off one by one as the rest of the class chants the words. Additionally, try putting this poem on a chart and, with each verse, cover another number word with *whoosh!* Pair this poem with the picture book *Firefighters A to Z* by Chris Demarest (2000).

fold here

# Five Little Leaves

Five little leaves so bright and gay

Were dancing about on a tree one day.

The wind came blowing through the town,

Oooooo . . . oooooo.

One little leaf came tumbling down.

May be photocopied for classroom use. ©2018 by Irene C. Fountas and Gay Su Pinnell from *Sing a Song of Poetry, Grade 1*. Portsmouth, NH: Heinemann.

**SUGGESTION:** Create a very windy classroom by asking children to make arm motions and *oooooo* sounds to represent leaves blowing in the wind. As they become familiar with the words, use this verse as a countdown rhyme. Five children may represent leaves, with one *tumbling* off the tree at the end of each stanza while the rest of the class recites and makes the appropriate movements and sounds. At the end, the last line changes to: *The last little leaf came tumbling down.* Vary the poem's last line to say *The first, The second,* and so forth.

# Five Little Mice

Five little mice came out to play,

Gathering crumbs along the way.

Out came pussycat sleek and fat,

Four little mice went scampering back.

ACTIONS:

Five little mice came out to play, [*one hand holding up five fingers*]

Gathering crumbs along the way. [*other hand comes out with fingers wiggling*]

Out came pussycat sleek and fat, [*cup first hand like a mouth*]

Four little mice went scampering back. [*cupped hand chases wiggling fingers behind back*]

SUGGESTION: You can use this rhyme as a hand play or choose five mice and one cat to act out the poem as the rest of the class recites. One mouse disappears in each stanza, until no little mice scamper anywhere.

fold here

May be photocopied for classroom use. ©2018 by Irene C. Fountas and Gay Su Pinnell from *Sing a Song of Poetry, Grade 1*. Portsmouth, NH: Heinemann.

# Five Little Sparrows

Five little sparrows
High in a tree.

The first one says,
"What do I see?"

The second one says,
"I see the street."

The third one says,
"And seeds to eat."

The fourth one says,
"The seeds are wheat."

The fifth one says,
"Tweet, tweet. Tweet, tweet."

May be photocopied for classroom use. ©2018 by Irene C. Fountas and Gay Su Pinnell from *Sing a Song of Poetry, Grade 1*. Portsmouth, NH: Heinemann.

fold here

**SUGGESTION:** The whole class can play the role of narrator while five different children read the dialogue. Have them read only the words in quotation marks. After children know the poem, they can locate words with /ee/.

# Five Little Speckled Frogs

Five little speckled frogs

Sitting on a speckled log

Eating some most delicious bugs.

Yum! Yum!

One jumped into the pool

Where it was nice and cool.

Now there are four little speckled frogs.

Burr-ump!

May be photocopied for classroom use. ©2018 by Irene C. Fountas and Gay Su Pinnell from *Sing a Song of Poetry, Grade 1*. Portsmouth, NH: Heinemann.

fold here

**SUGGESTION:** Continue this countdown poem with four more verses, beginning with one fewer frog each time. Children will vie to be one of the five speckled frogs who eat delicious bugs and jump into the pool. This is a great game song to sing or recite. In the end when there are no more little speckled frogs, the game can start again.

# Four Seasons

Spring is showery, flowery, bowery.

Summer is hoppy, croppy, poppy.

Autumn is wheezy, sneezy, freezy.

Winter is slippy, drippy, nippy.

May be photocopied for classroom use. ©2018 by Irene C. Fountas and Gay Su Pinnell from *Sing a Song of Poetry, Grade 1*. Portsmouth, NH: Heinemann.

fold here

**SUGGESTION:** Invite children to talk about how the words describe the seasons and why they might have been chosen. You may need to explain that *bowery* means "trees." Have children illustrate the various seasons by relying on the descriptions given in the poem.

# Fresh Fried Fish

Fresh fried fish

Fish fresh fried,

Fried fresh fish,

Fish fried fresh.

May be photocopied for classroom use. ©2018 by Irene C. Fountas and Gay Su Pinnell from *Sing a Song of Poetry, Grade 1*. Portsmouth, NH: Heinemann.

fold here

**SUGGESTION:** Have children say this tongue twister slowly at first and then faster. After they know the poem and are looking at a written version, have them compare words that start with *f* and *fr*.

# Giddyup, Horsie

Giddyup, horsie, to the fair.

What'll we buy when we get there?

A penny apple and a penny pear

Giddyup, horsie, to the fair.

Up the wooden hill to Blanket Fair,

What shall we have when we get there?

A bucket full of water, a pennyworth of hay,

Giddyup, horsie, all the way.

May be photocopied for classroom use. ©2018 by Irene C. Fountas and Gay Su Pinnell from *Sing a Song of Poetry, Grade 1*. Portsmouth, NH: Heinemann.

fold here

**SUGGESTION:** Talk with children about how people used to ride horses to town instead of driving or taking buses. Ask them to guess what *pennyworth* might mean.

# Go 'Round and 'Round the Village

Go 'round and 'round the village,
Go 'round and 'round the village,
Go 'round and 'round the village,
As we have done before.

Go in and out the window,
Go in and out the window,
Go in and out the window,
As we have done before.

Stand and face your partner,
Stand and face your partner,
Stand and face your partner,
As we have done before.

Follow him [her] to London,
Follow him [her] to London,
Follow him [her] to London,
As we have done before.

Now shake his [her] hand and leave him [her],
Now shake his [her] hand and leave him [her],
Now shake his [her] hand and leave him [her],
As we have done before.

May be photocopied for classroom use. ©2018 by Irene C. Fountas and Gay Su Pinnell from *Sing a Song of Poetry, Grade 1*. Portsmouth, NH: Heinemann.

**SUGGESTION:** Have children stand in a circle. One child is "it" and runs around the circle while the others sing. On the second verse, children in the circle raise their arms to make windows while "it" goes in and out between them. On the third verse, "it" chooses a partner and they both face each other to bow. On the fourth verse, the partners join hands and skip around the circle. They go back inside the circle on the fifth verse to shake hands, and then the class starts again with a new child chosen to be "it."

fold here

# Going to the Fair

I know where I'm going.

I'm going to the fair

To see a pretty lady

With flowers in her hair.


So shake it, _____, shake it.

Shake it if you can.

Shake it like a milkshake.

Shake it if you can.

May be photocopied for classroom use. ©2018 by Irene C. Fountas and Gay Su Pinnell from *Sing a Song of Poetry, Grade 1*. Portsmouth, NH: Heinemann.

**SUGGESTION:** Invite children to form a circle and sing the first verse. If you use the second verse, tap one child on the shoulder to stand in the middle and dance, returning to the circle quickly as verse one starts again. You can choose to insert a child's name where the blank line appears or just add an additional *shake it*.

# Good Morning, Mrs. Hen

Good morning, Mrs. Hen.

How many chickens have you got?

Madam, I've got ten;

Four of them are yellow,

Four of them are brown,

And two of them are speckled red,

The nicest in the town.

May be photocopied for classroom use. ©2018 by Irene C. Fountas and Gay Su Pinnell from *Sing a Song of Poetry, Grade 1*. Portsmouth, NH: Heinemann.

fold here

**SUGGESTION:** Divide children into two groups to read the parts of Madam and Mrs. Hen. Explain that *Madam* means "Mrs. or lady." You can make this poem interesting by playing with the numbers. Children can work with ten eggs on a feltboard or magnet board by making different combinations that add up to ten. Consider pairing this poem with "The Clever Hen" (also in this volume).

# Good Morning Song

Good morning, good morning, good morning to you,

Good morning, good morning, good morning to you,

Our day is beginning, there's so much to do,

So, good morning, good morning, good morning to you.

May be photocopied for classroom use. ©2018 by Irene C. Fountas and Gay Su Pinnell from *Sing a Song of Poetry, Grade 1*. Portsmouth, NH: Heinemann.

**SUGGESTION:** Use this as a routine "morning" song. It will take only a few minutes. After children learn the song, have them read it in print. Help them notice the *-ing* words.

# The Grand Old Duke of York

Oh, the grand old duke of York,

He had ten thousand men.

He marched them up to the top of the hill,

And marched them down again.


Oh, when you're up, you're up,

And when you're down, you're down,

And when you're only halfway up,

You're neither up nor down.

May be photocopied for classroom use. ©2018 by Irene C. Fountas and Gay Su Pinnell from *Sing a Song of Poetry, Grade 1*. Portsmouth, NH: Heinemann.

**SUGGESTION:** This is a good marching song. Children can march in place as they recite the first verse. During the second verse, they can match actions to the words line by line: stand up, crouch down, stand halfway up, and then jump up and down.

fold here

# Handy Pandy

Handy Pandy, Jack-a-dandy,

Loves plum cake and sugar candy.

He bought some at the grocer's shop

And out he came, hop, hop, hop.

VARIATIONS:

Handy Pandy, Jack-a-dandy,
Loves carrot cake and chocolate candy.
He bought some at the grocery store
And he was happy ever more.

Handy Pandy, sugar candy,
French almond rock;
Bread and butter for your supper
That is all your mother's got.

May be photocopied for classroom use. ©2018 by Irene C. Fountas and Gay Su Pinnell from *Sing a Song of Poetry, Grade 1*. Portsmouth, NH: Heinemann.

fold here

**SUGGESTION:** There are some great food words in this poem: *plum cake*, *sugar candy*, and so on. Present the variations (you can substitute healthier foods), and then ask children what they would buy at the grocery store. Invite them to illustrate the poem based on the food they would buy.

# Hanky Panky

Down by the banks of the Hanky Panky,

Where the bullfrogs jump from bank to banky

With an Eep! Eep! Ope! Ope!

Knee-flop-i-dilly and kerplop!

May be photocopied for classroom use. ©2018 by Irene C. Fountas and Gay Su Pinnell from *Sing a Song of Poetry, Grade 1*. Portsmouth, NH: Heinemann.

fold here

**SUGGESTION:** Children enjoy the nonsense words in this poem. Help them discuss how words can make you think of real noises by suggesting the sounds they represent, such as *purr, buzz, fizz,* and *crackle.*

# Hark, Hark!

Hark, hark! The dogs do bark,

Beggars are coming to town;

Some in rags, some in tags,

And some in velvet gowns.

May be photocopied for classroom use. ©2018 by Irene C. Fountas and Gay Su Pinnell from *Sing a Song of Poetry, Grade 1*. Portsmouth, NH: Heinemann.

**SUGGESTION:** Assign four different groups of children for each line. You may want to explain that the word *beggars* sometimes meant "people who dressed up and gave performances."

# Hey Diddle Dout

Hey diddle dout,

My candle's out,

My little maid's not at home;

Saddle the hog,

And bridle the dog,

And fetch my little maid home.

May be photocopied for classroom use. ©2018 by Irene C. Fountas and Gay Su Pinnell from *Sing a Song of Poetry, Grade 1.* Portsmouth, NH: Heinemann.

fold here

**SUGGESTION:** Invite some children to beat out the rhythm with a stick or drum while the others say the poem. Some archaic language in this poem like *little maid*, *saddle*, and *bridle* may require definition and context.

# Hickory, Dickory, Dare

Hickory, dickory, dare,

The pig flew up in the air.

The man in brown

Soon brought him down,

Hickory, dickory, dare.

May be photocopied for classroom use. ©2018 by Irene C. Fountas and Gay Su Pinnell from *Sing a Song of Poetry, Grade 1*. Portsmouth, NH: Heinemann.

**SUGGESTION:** Children will enjoy comparing the events, characters, and words in this poem to those in "Hickory, Dickory, Dock" and "Hickory, Dickory, Dean."

# Hickory, Dickory, Dean

Hickory, dickory, dean,

The dog was very clean.

The cat was fine

To sit and dine,

Hickory, dickory, dean.

May be photocopied for classroom use. ©2018 by Irene C. Fountas and Gay Su Pinnell from *Sing a Song of Poetry, Grade 1*. Portsmouth, NH: Heinemann.

**SUGGESTION:** After reading "Hickory, Dickory, Dare" and "Hickory, Dickory, Dean," invite children to discuss how changing the ending part of a word makes a new word.

fold here

# A Horse and a Flea
# and Three Blind Mice

A horse and a flea and three blind mice

Sat on a curbstone eating ice.

The horse he slipped and sat on the flea.

The flea said, "Whoops, there's a horse on me!"

May be photocopied for classroom use. ©2018 by Irene C. Fountas and Gay Su Pinnell from *Sing a Song of Poetry, Grade 1*. Portsmouth, NH: Heinemann.

fold here   **SUGGESTION:** Children will enjoy the funny images in the poem. Emphasize expression in saying the last line. You can also point out the quotation marks and exclamation point and discuss what they indicate.

# Horsie, Horsie

Horsie, horsie, don't you stop,

Just let your feet go clippety clop.

Your tail goes swish and the wheels go 'round,

Giddyup, you're homeward bound.

May be photocopied for classroom use. ©2018 by Irene C. Fountas and Gay Su Pinnell from *Sing a Song of Poetry, Grade 1*. Portsmouth, NH: Heinemann.

fold here

**UGGESTION:** Children can come up with the sound effects and motions for this poem: tapping fingernails or clapping for *clippity clop*, moving hands quickly for *swish*, and revolving both hands around each other to show how the *wheels go 'round*. Have children locate words that sound like real noises.

# How Much Dew?

How much dew

Does a dewdrop drop

If dewdrops

Do drop dew?


They drop the dew

That they do,

When dewdrops

Do drop dew.

May be photocopied for classroom use. ©2018 by Irene C. Fountas and Gay Su Pinnell from *Sing a Song of Poetry, Grade 1*. Portsmouth, NH: Heinemann.

**SUGGESTION:** Talk about dewdrops and show children a photograph to help them identify dew in the morning. Even if they don't fully understand the concept, children can enjoy the nonsense. Compare *do* and *dew* and read as if these words rhyme. If children enjoy the tongue twister, introduce them to others in this volume ("I Saw a Saw" and "Peter Piper" are two examples).

# I Had a Little Brother

I had a little brother

No bigger than my thumb;

I put him in the coffee pot

Where he rattled like a drum.

May be photocopied for classroom use. ©2018 by Irene C. Fountas and Gay Su Pinnell from *Sing a Song of Poetry, Grade 1*. Portsmouth, NH: Heinemann.

**SUGGESTION:** Say the poem with strong rhythm and a fast pace. Show children that *thumb* and *drum* rhyme even though they look different at the end. Then have them locate double consonants.

fold here

# I Had a Little Rooster

I had a little rooster by the barnyard gate,

That little rooster was my playmate.

That little rooster went cock-a-doodle-doo,

Dee-doodle-dee, doodle-dee, doodle-dee-doo.

I had a little cat by the barnyard gate,

That little cat was my playmate.

That little cat went meow, meow, meow,

That little rooster went cock-a-doodle-doo,

Dee-doodle-dee, doodle-dee, doodle-dee-doo.

I had a little dog by the barnyard gate,

That little dog was my playmate.

That little dog went arf, arf, arf,

That little cat went meow, meow, meow,

That little rooster went cock-a-doodle-doo,

Dee-doodle-dee, doodle-dee, doodle-dee-doo.

May be photocopied for classroom use. ©2018 by Irene C. Fountas and Gay Su Pinnell from *Sing a Song of Poetry, Grade 1*. Portsmouth, NH: Heinemann.

**SUGGESTION:** This cumulative poem is a great song to sing and could be the basis for a lively production number. Find the melody on the Internet. Then invite preassigned children to make the sounds of different animals while the rest of the class recites or sings the poem. Consider adding more animals to the poem: e.g., *cow, sheep, duck,* or *pig*. This will challenge children to stretch their imaginations and memories.

# I Had a Loose Tooth

I had a loose tooth,

A wiggly, jiggly loose tooth.

I had a loose tooth,

A-hanging by a thread.

I pulled my loose tooth,

My wiggly, jiggly loose tooth.

Put it under my pillow,

And then I went to bed.

The fairy took my loose tooth,

My wiggly, jiggly loose tooth.

And now I have a quarter,

And a hole in my head.

ACTIONS:

I had a loose tooth,

A wiggly, jiggly loose tooth.
[*pretend to wiggle a tooth as if it were in the mouth*]

I had a loose tooth,

A-hanging by a thread. [*hold hand up as if holding a tooth on a string*]

I pulled my loose tooth,
[*pretend to pull tooth*]

My wiggly, jiggly loose tooth.
[*pretend to shake tooth in palm of hand*]

Put it under my pillow,

And then I went to bed. [*put two hands together and lean head on them*]

The fairy took my loose tooth,
[*pretend to hold up tooth*]

My wiggly, jiggly loose tooth.
[*pretend to shake tooth in palm of hand*]

And now I have a quarter, [*hold palm out*]

And a hole in my head. [*point to jaw*]

May be photocopied for classroom use. ©2018 by Irene C. Fountas and Gay Su Pinnell from *Sing a Song of Poetry, Grade 1*. Portsmouth, NH: Heinemann.

**SUGGESTION:** Losing a tooth is a big event in a primary classroom. Children are compelled to talk about how the tooth finally fell out. Revisit this poem and the accompanying actions each time a child loses a tooth. Help children to notice double consonants and vowels, as well as the -*ly* endings.

fold here

# I Have a Little Cough

I have a little cough, sir,

In my little chest sir,

Every time I cough, sir,

It leaves a little pain, sir,

Cough, cough, cough, cough,

There it is again, sir.

May be photocopied for classroom use. ©2018 by Irene C. Fountas and Gay Su Pinnell from *Sing a Song of Poetry, Grade 1*. Portsmouth, NH: Heinemann.

**SUGGESTION:** Children will have fun acting out the repetitive coughing action in this simple verse. After they are familiar with the words and have had fun coughing, briefly discuss the words *sir* and *ma'am*. With the verse on chart paper, or in a pocket chart, you can replace *sir* with *ma'am* and recite the new version together.

# I Have Two Eyes

I have two eyes to see with,

I have two feet to run,

I have two hands to wave with,

And nose I have but one.

I have two ears to hear with,

And a tongue to say "Good day."

May be photocopied for classroom use. ©2018 by Irene C. Fountas and Gay Su Pinnell from *Sing a Song of Poetry, Grade 1*. Portsmouth, NH: Heinemann.

ACTIONS:

I have two eyes to see with, [*sitting, point with both hands to eyes*]

I have two feet to run, [*lift one foot, then the other*]

I have two hands to wave with, [*wave with both hands*]

And nose I have but one. [*point to nose*]

I have two ears to hear with, [*both hands behind ears*]

And a tongue to say "Good day." [*stand up on* "Good day"]

SUGGESTION: Give children reproducible copies of the poem and have them draw a self-portrait to illustrate it. They have to be sure to include everything mentioned in the poem.

fold here

# I Know a Little Puppy

I know a little puppy; he hasn't any tail.

He isn't very chubby; he's skinny as a rail.

Although he is a puppy, he'll never be a hound.

They sell him at the shop for 30 cents a pound.

Bow-wow, wow-wow, wow-wow, wow.

HOT DOG!

May be photocopied for classroom use. ©2018 by Irene C. Fountas and Gay Su Pinnell from *Sing a Song of Poetry, Grade 1*. Portsmouth, NH: Heinemann.

**SUGGESTION:** This poem is really a riddle. Keep the last two lines covered. After the first four lines, have children guess what kind of puppy is in the poem, and uncover the last two lines to check predictions. They can talk about the two meanings of *dog*.

# I Know Something

I know something I won't tell.

Three little monkeys in a peanut shell.

One can read and one can write,

And one can fly a great big kite.

May be photocopied for classroom use. ©2018 by Irene C. Fountas and Gay Su Pinnell from *Sing a Song of Poetry, Grade 1*. Portsmouth, NH: Heinemann.

**SUGGESTION:** Make a triptych by folding a piece of paper into thirds. Children love illustrating one monkey in each space. This poem leaves lots of room for both monkeyshines and creative thought.

fold here

# I Love the Mountains

I love the mountains.

I love the rolling hills.

I love the flowers.

I love the daffodils.

I love the fireside

When all the lights are low.

Boom-de-otta, boom-de-otta,

Boom-de-otta, boom-de-otta.

May be photocopied for classroom use. ©2018 by Irene C. Fountas and Gay Su Pinnell from *Sing a Song of Poetry, Grade 1*. Portsmouth, NH: Heinemann.

**SUGGESTION:** Find this song on the Internet and teach children the melody. Then invite them to sing it as a round, with one group starting after the other group has sung the first two lines. Alternatively, have two groups sing or say alternate lines, following quickly along. Or have one group say *Boom-de-otta* continually while the others sing the whole song. Pair this verse with the picture book *I Love the Mountains: A Traditional Song* by John Archambault and David Plummer (1998).

# I Never Had a Dog
# that Could Talk

I never had a dog that could talk,

Or a cat that could sing a song,

Or a pony that could on two legs walk,

And keep it up all the day long;

Or a pig that could whistle a merry tune,

Or a hen that could dance a jig,

Or a cow that could jump clear over the moon,

Or a musical guinea pig.

May be photocopied for classroom use. ©2018 by Irene C. Fountas and Gay Su Pinnell from *Sing a Song of Poetry, Grade 1*. Portsmouth, NH: Heinemann.

**SUGGESTION:** Invite children to talk about what makes this poem funny. They can substitute names of other animals or their pets, or they can think of other funny characteristics.

fold here

# I Saw a Saw

I saw a saw in Arkansas,

That would outsaw

Any saw I ever saw,

And if you have a saw

That will outsaw the saw

I saw in Arkansas

Let me see your saw.

May be photocopied for classroom use. ©2018 by Irene C. Fountas and Gay Su Pinnell from *Sing a Song of Poetry, Grade 1*. Portsmouth, NH: Heinemann.

fold here

**SUGGESTION:** Invite children to think about the two meanings of the word *saw*. (They may not know that *saw* also means "tool.") Point out that *Arkansas* rhymes with *saw* but is spelled differently.

# I Saw Three Ships

I saw three ships come sailing by,
Come sailing by, come sailing by;
I saw three ships come sailing by,
On New Year's Day in the morning.

And what do you think was in them then,
Was in them then, was in them then?
And what do you think was in them then,
On New Year's Day in the morning?

Three pretty girls were in them then,
Were in them then, were in them then,
Three pretty girls were in them then,
On New Year's Day in the morning.

And one could whistle and one could sing,
And one could play the violin;
Such joy there was at my wedding,
On New Year's Day in the morning.

May be photocopied for classroom use. ©2018 by Irene C. Fountas and Gay Su Pinnell from *Sing a Song of Poetry, Grade 1*. Portsmouth, NH: Heinemann.

**SUGGESTION:** Substitute New Year's Day for other holidays (Valentine's Day, etc.). Children love reciting this poem. After they are familiar with it, invite them to divide into four groups—one for each stanza—and illustrate their respective lines.

fold here

# I Went Downtown

I went downtown
To see Mrs. Brown.

She gave me a nickel
To buy a pickle.

The pickle was sour,
She gave me a flower.

The flower was dead,
She gave me a thread.

The thread was thin,
She gave me a pin.

The pin was sharp,
She gave me a harp.

And the harp began to sing—

Minnie and a minnie
And a ha ha ha!

May be photocopied for classroom use. ©2018 by Irene C. Fountas and Gay Su Pinnell from *Sing a Song of Poetry, Grade 1*. Portsmouth, NH: Heinemann.

fold here

**SUGGESTION:** This poem reinforces rhyming words. Children can predict each new item given by Mrs. Brown based on the word at the end of the preceding line, as well as create their own rhymes. Assign groups to read each verse; save the last verse for the class to read together.

# I Would If I Could

I would

If I could!

But I can't,

So I won't!

May be photocopied for classroom use. ©2018 by Irene C. Fountas and Gay Su Pinnell from *Sing a Song of Poetry, Grade 1*. Portsmouth, NH: Heinemann.

**SUGGESTION:** This poem doesn't rhyme but depends on rhythm and juxtaposition of words for its appeal. Children will enjoy reciting it emphatically. They can play a game in which one child poses a silly question (such as *Would you like to eat worms?*) and the rest say the poem as an answer.

fold here

# If I Had a Donkey

If I had a donkey and he wouldn't go,

Do you think I'd whip him?

Oh, no, no!

I'd put him in the barn,

And give him some corn,

The best little donkey that ever was born.

May be photocopied for classroom use. ©2018 by Irene C. Fountas and Gay Su Pinnell from *Sing a Song of Poetry, Grade 1*. Portsmouth, NH: Heinemann.

fold here

**SUGGESTION:** Talk with children about the days when people depended on horses and donkeys to carry them and pull carts. You could whip your animal or treat it kindly. In this poem, the writer wants to treat the donkey well.

# If You're Happy and You Know It

If you're happy and you know it,

Clap your hands.

If you're happy and you know it,

Clap your hands.

If you're happy and you know it,

Then your face will surely show it.

If you're happy and you know it,

Clap your hands.

May be photocopied for classroom use. ©2018 by Irene C. Fountas and Gay Su Pinnell from *Sing a Song of Poetry, Grade 1.* Portsmouth, NH: Heinemann.

**SUGGESTION:** Do the actions while singing or saying the poem. Children enjoy making up new rhymes and motions together, such as *Stomp your feet, Stand and cheer,* and *Shout hooray!*

fold here

# I'd Like to Be a Lighthouse

*by Rachel Field*

I'd like to be a lighthouse

All scrubbed and painted white.

I'd like to be a lighthouse

And stay awake all night

To keep my eye on everything

That sails my patch of sea;

I'd like to be a lighthouse

With the ships all watching me.

May be photocopied for classroom use. ©2018 by Irene C. Fountas and Gay Su Pinnell from *Sing a Song of Poetry, Grade 1*. Portsmouth, NH: Heinemann.

**SUGGESTION:** Select one child to pretend to be the lighthouse. Give him or her a flashlight. Invite the rest of the class to sit in a circle and ask the lighthouse to stand in the middle. Dim or turn off the classroom lights. While the seated children recite the poem, ask them to gently wave their arms, pretending to be the sea. Have the lighthouse spin in circles while shining the flashlight on the sea. When the poem ends, have the lighthouse stop moving; the seated child in the light can then switch places with the lighthouse. Have the class recite the poem again and again.

# I'm a Little Teapot

I'm a little teapot,

Short and stout,

Here is my handle,

Here is my spout.

When I get all steamed up,

Hear me shout,

"Tip me over

And pour me out!"

ACTIONS:

I'm a little teapot,
Short and stout,
Here is my handle, [*one hand on hip*]
Here is my spout. [*other hand pointed outward*]
When I get all steamed up,
I just shout:
Tip me over [*lean sideways to pour from spout*]
And pour me out!

May be photocopied for classroom use. ©2018 by Irene C. Fountas and Gay Su Pinnell from *Sing a Song of Poetry, Grade 1*. Portsmouth, NH: Heinemann.

fold here

**SUGGESTION:** Many children may already know this old favorite and will enjoy singing it while they act it out. Share a printed version, and have them highlight all the rhyming -*out* words. Discuss how changing the beginning part of a word makes a new word.

# It's Raining

It's raining, it's pouring,

The old man is snoring;

He went to bed and bumped his head

And couldn't get up in the morning.

May be photocopied for classroom use. ©2018 by Irene C. Fountas and Gay Su Pinnell from *Sing a Song of Poetry, Grade 1*. Portsmouth, NH: Heinemann.

fold here

**SUGGESTION:** This traditional verse has a somewhat mournful tone, but children enjoy saying or singing it. You can find the tune on the Internet. Revisit the poem on days when the weather matches. Try tagging two more lines on the end: *Rain, rain, go away. / Come again some other day.*

# The Itsy, Bitsy Spider

The itsy, bitsy spider

Climbed up the waterspout.

Down came the rain

And washed the spider out.

Out came the sun

And dried up all the rain.

And the itsy, bitsy spider

Climbed up the spout again.

ACTIONS:

The itsy, bitsy spider [*touch pointer finger to thumb*]

Climbed up the waterspout. [*walk hands up by switching between pointer fingers and thumbs*]

Down came the rain [*make rain motions by fluttering fingers down*]

And washed the spider out.

Out came the sun [*hands above head making a circle*]

And dried up all the rain.

And the itsy, bitsy spider [*repeat spider walking motion*]

Climbed up the spout again.

SUGGESTION: Sing the song with actions. Have children substitute other words for *itsy, bitsy* that mean "small", like *eensy, weensy; teeny, tiny;* or *wee, little.*

May be photocopied for classroom use. ©2018 by Irene C. Fountas and Gay Su Pinnell from *Sing a Song of Poetry, Grade 1*. Portsmouth, NH: Heinemann.

fold here

# I've Got a Dog
# as Thin as a Rail

I've got a dog as thin as a rail,

He's got fleas all over his tail;

Every time his tail goes flop,

The fleas on the bottom all hop to the top.

May be photocopied for classroom use. ©2018 by Irene C. Fountas and Gay Su Pinnell from *Sing a Song of Poetry, Grade 1*. Portsmouth, NH: Heinemann.

fold here

**SUGGESTION:** This verse has a predictable structure children can use to create other rhymes: *I've got a _____, as _____ as a _____.* See what children can come up with, and have them make an illustrated class book to showcase their efforts.

# Jack, Be Nimble

Jack, be nimble,

Jack, be quick,

Jack, jump over

The candlestick.


Jack, be nimble,

Quick as a fox,

Jack, jump over

This little box.


**ADDITIONAL VERSES**

Jack, be nimble,
Jack, cut a caper,
Jack, jump over
This piece of paper.

Jack, be nimble,
Jack, be fair,
Jack, jump over
This little chair.

May be photocopied for classroom use. ©2018 by Irene C. Fountas and Gay Su Pinnell from *Sing a Song of Poetry, Grade 1*. Portsmouth, NH: Heinemann.

fold here

**SUGGESTION:** Children enjoy discovering the meaning of the word *nimble*. Class members may take turns jumping over a real or imaginary candlestick. (Candlesticks are easily made from small paper plates, short paper rolls, glue, and paper scraps.) A set of blocks or other small obstruction can be jumped instead. Different names can be substituted for *Jack*. Create new verses in which the second and fourth lines rhyme. Outside, let class members chant the words and jump over a rope held by two children. If everyone makes it over one height, raise the rope.

# Jack-in-the-box

Jack-in-the-box,

All shut up tight;

Not a breath of air,

Not a ray of light.

How tired he must be

Down in a heap;

We'll open the lid

And up he will leap.

May be photocopied for classroom use. ©2018 by Irene C. Fountas and Gay Su Pinnell from *Sing a Song of Poetry, Grade 1*. Portsmouth, NH: Heinemann.

fold here

**SUGGESTION:** Have children begin saying the verse while they are sitting down and jump up on the final line. Talk with them about what a jack-in-the-box is, and ask them to imagine being scrunched up inside a box.

# Johnny Appleseed

Oh, the earth is good to me,

And so I thank the earth,

For giving me the things I need:

The sun, the rain, and the apple seed.

The earth is good to me.

May be photocopied for classroom use. ©2018 by Irene C. Fountas and Gay Su Pinnell from *Sing a Song of Poetry, Grade 1*. Portsmouth, NH: Heinemann.

**SUGGESTION:** Children may enjoy hearing the story of Johnny Appleseed who traveled all his life planting apple trees. They can also talk about how the sun and rain help the tiny seeds grow into trees.

fold here

# Ladies and Gentlemen

Ladies and gentlemen,

Come to supper—

Hot boiled beans

And very good butter.

May be photocopied for classroom use. ©2018 by Irene C. Fountas and Gay Su Pinnell from *Sing a Song of Poetry, Grade 1*. Portsmouth, NH: Heinemann.

fold here

**SUGGESTION:** Children can talk about their favorite foods to have for supper (or they may call it dinner) and substitute them in the poem. This poem does not rhyme, so the only consideration will be to match the number of syllables in the line. Trying words to see if they "sound right" will require children to say words and listen to syllables.

# The Lady and the Crocodile

She sailed away on a bright and sunny day,

On the back of a crocodile.

"You see," said she, "he's as tame as he can be;

I'll ride him down the Nile."

The croc winked his eye as she bade them all good-bye,

Wearing a happy smile.

At the end of the ride the lady was inside,

And the smile was on the crocodile!

May be photocopied for classroom use. ©2018 by Irene C. Fountas and Gay Su Pinnell from *Sing a Song of Poetry, Grade 1*. Portsmouth, NH: Heinemann.

**SUGGESTION:** As children become familiar with this poem, it can be fun to present it with "Crocodile" (also in this volume). Children can break into two groups, each learning one of the poems. After they add pantomime movements, they can perform for the other group. Ask children to retell the story, emphasizing that it's funny because no one would ever think of riding a crocodile.

# The Lady with the Alligator Purse

Miss Lucy had a baby,

She named him Tiny Tim.

She put him in the bathtub

To see if he could swim.

He drank up all the water,

He ate up all the soap,

He tried to eat the bathtub,

But it wouldn't go down his throat.

Miss Lucy called the doctor,

Miss Lucy called the nurse,

Miss Lucy called the lady

With the alligator purse.

In walked the doctor,

In walked the nurse,

In walked the lady

With the alligator purse.

*continued*

May be photocopied for classroom use. ©2018 by Irene C. Fountas and Gay Su Pinnell from *Sing a Song of Poetry, Grade 1*. Portsmouth, NH: Heinemann.

fold here

126

"Measles," said the doctor,

"Chicken pox," said the nurse,

"Mumps," said the lady

With the alligator purse.

"Penicillin," said the doctor,

"Aspirin," said the nurse,

"Pizza," said the lady

With the alligator purse.

A dime for the doctor,

A nickel for the nurse,

Nothing for the lady

With the alligator purse.

Out walked the doctor,

Out walked the nurse,

Out walked the lady

With the alligator purse.

May be photocopied for classroom use. ©2018 by Irene C. Fountas and Gay Su Pinnell from *Sing a Song of Poetry, Grade 1*. Portsmouth, NH: Heinemann.

**SUGGESTION:** Children love to take turns acting out this rhythmic poem while the rest of the group forms a circle and chants the words. Invite children to clap while reciting the poem to help emphasize the rhyming words.

fold here

# Lavender's Blue

Lavender's blue,

Dilly, dilly,

Lavender's green.

When I am King,

Dilly, dilly,

You shall be Queen.

Who told you so,

Dilly, dilly,

Who told you so?

'Twas my own heart,

Dilly, dilly,

That told me so.

May be photocopied for classroom use. ©2018 by Irene C. Fountas and Gay Su Pinnell from *Sing a Song of Poetry, Grade 1*. Portsmouth, NH: Heinemann.

**SUGGESTION:** This is an old nonsense song. It's included on John Langstaff's CD *Jackfish and More Songs for Singing Children* (2001). Make an illustrated poetry chart with your students, or use tagboard strips and a pocket chart to build the poem together. Assign a small group to read or sing *Dilly, dilly*. Create two-syllable substitutes for *Dilly, dilly*: e.g., *Ducky, ducky*.

# The Lion and the Unicorn

The Lion and the Unicorn

Were fighting for the crown,

The Lion beat the Unicorn,

All around the town.

Some gave them white bread,

Some gave them brown,

Some gave them plum-cake,

And sent them out of town.

May be photocopied for classroom use. ©2018 by Irene C. Fountas and Gay Su Pinnell from *Sing a Song of Poetry, Grade 1*. Portsmouth, NH: Heinemann.

fold here

**SUGGESTION:** Check on children's knowledge of the animals *lion* and *unicorn*. Even if children are unfamiliar, they can enjoy this rhyme. They may also be interested to know that these animals are symbols of the United Kingdom. Show children on a map which countries make up the United Kingdom. Then together as a class, substitute *lion* and/or *unicorn* for other animals. After they know the poem, invite children to say and look at the words *crown, town,* and *brown* as examples of rhyming words.

# Listen to the Tree Bear

Listen to the tree bear

Crying in the night

Crying for his mamma

In the pale moonlight.

What will his mamma do

When she hears him cry?

She'll tuck him in a cocoa-pod

And sing a lullaby.

May be photocopied for classroom use. ©2018 by Irene C. Fountas and Gay Su Pinnell from *Sing a Song of Poetry, Grade 1*. Portsmouth, NH: Heinemann.

**SUGGESTION:** After children are familiar with the words of this poem, work with them on emphasizing the strong natural rhythm as they practice reciting or performing. Encourage them to change their inflection as they follow the cadence. Also, invite children to talk about what kinds of bears like to hang out in trees: e.g., pandas.

# Little Betty Blue

Little Betty Blue

Lost her holiday shoe.

What will little Betty do?

Why, give her another

To match the other,

And then she can walk out in two.

May be photocopied for classroom use. ©2018 by Irene C. Fountas and Gay Su Pinnell from *Sing a Song of Poetry, Grade 1.* Portsmouth, NH: Heinemann.

**SUGGESTION:** Divide the poem into two parts of three lines each. Have groups of children take turns reciting each half. Invite children to substitute names and come up with other lost items that come in pairs: e.g., *sock, glove, earmuff,* and *earring.* Change Betty's last name to make them rhyme.

fold here

# Little Bird

Once I saw a little bird

Come hop, hop, hop;

So I cried, "Little bird,

Will you stop, stop, stop?"


I was going to the window

To say, "How do you do?"

But he shook his little tail,

And far away he flew.

May be photocopied for classroom use. ©2018 by Irene C. Fountas and Gay Su Pinnell from *Sing a Song of Poetry, Grade 1*. Portsmouth, NH: Heinemann.

**SUGGESTION:** Assign one child to read the material in quotation marks while others say the rest. This is a good poem to point out the function of quotation marks. Alternatively, have children substitute words for *cried* to increase their awareness of possibilities: e.g., *said, shouted, called,* or *whispered.*

# Little Blue Ben

Little blue Ben, who lives in the glen,

Keeps a blue cat and one blue hen

Who lays blue eggs a score and ten.

Where shall I find my little blue Ben?

May be photocopied for classroom use. ©2018 by Irene C. Fountas and Gay Su Pinnell from *Sing a Song of Poetry, Grade 1*. Portsmouth, NH: Heinemann.

fold here

**SUGGESTION:** Explain to children that the word *glen* means "narrow valley" and that *a score and ten* actually means a number; *score* means "the number 20." The hen lays a lot of eggs! Invite children to play with the poem by rotating through different colors. Once they are familiar with the poem, children can practice identifying rhyming words with the phonogram *-en*.

# Little Bo-Peep

Little Bo-Peep has lost her sheep,

And can't tell where to find them;

Leave them alone, and they'll come home,

Wagging their tails behind them.


Little Bo-Peep fell fast asleep

And dreamed she heard them bleating;

But when she woke, it was all a joke,

For they were still a-fleeting.


Then up she took her little crook,

And vowed that she would find them;

What was her joy to see them there,

Wagging their tails behind them.

May be photocopied for classroom use. ©2018 by Irene C. Fountas and Gay Su Pinnell from *Sing a Song of Poetry, Grade 1*. Portsmouth, NH: Heinemann.

**SUGGESTION:** This poem lends itself to creating a three-page class book (one verse on each page) or individual books that children illustrate. Explain that a shepherd's *crook* is "a long stick with a hooked end" that Little Bo-Peep uses to pull sheep into line. Also explain that to *vow* means "to promise" and that *bleating* is "the crying sound that sheep make."

# Little Boy Blue

Little Boy Blue,

Come blow your horn.

The sheep's in the meadow,

The cow's in the corn.

Where is the boy

Who looks after the sheep?

He's under the haystack

Fast asleep.

Will you wake him?

No, not I,

For if I do,

He's sure to cry.

May be photocopied for classroom use. ©2018 by Irene C. Fountas and Gay Su Pinnell from *Sing a Song of Poetry, Grade 1*. Portsmouth, NH: Heinemann.

**SUGGESTION:** Invite children to get in groups and take turns reciting every other line. Then ask them to draw the scene; drawing will help children to decipher the poem's details. Pair this with Iona Opie and Rosemary Wells's picture book *Little Boy Blue* (1997).

fold here

# The Little Green Frog

Glack, gloon, went the little green frog one day.

Glack, gloon, went the little green frog.

Glack, gloon, went the little green frog one day.

And his eyes went glock, glack, gloon.

May be photocopied for classroom use. ©2018 by Irene C. Fountas and Gay Su Pinnell from *Sing a Song of Poetry, Grade 1.* Portsmouth, NH: Heinemann.

fold here

**SUGGESTION:** Substitute other noises that a frog might make. On the last line, have children make a circle with their fingers around their eyes. Work with them to show how changing the middle or end of a word makes a new word: e.g., *glack* to *glock* and *glock* to *gloon*.

# Little Mousie

See the little mousie

Creeping up the stair,

Looking for a warm nest.

There—oh, there!

May be photocopied for classroom use. ©2018 by Irene C. Fountas and Gay Su Pinnell from *Sing a Song of Poetry, Grade 1*. Portsmouth, NH: Heinemann.

fold here

**SUGGESTION:** After children know the words to this poem, have them add actions to make it a finger rhyme. Invite them to use two fingers to *creep* up their arm and find a *warm nest* in the crook of the elbow. Then have children create additional verses by substituting two-syllable animal names, such as *sparrow* or *gerbil*.

# Little Nancy Etticoat

Little Nancy Etticoat

With a white petticoat,

And a red nose;

She has no feet or hands,

The longer she stands,

The shorter she grows.

May be photocopied for classroom use. ©2018 by Irene C. Fountas and Gay Su Pinnell from *Sing a Song of Poetry, Grade 1*. Portsmouth, NH: Heinemann.

fold here

**SUGGESTION:** This poem is really a riddle. What is Little Nancy Etticoat? She's a candle! Draw a picture to give children a visual clue as they recite the poem, and invite them to guess the riddle's answer.

# Little Peter Rabbit

Little Peter Rabbit had a fly upon his nose.

Little Peter Rabbit had a fly upon his nose.

Little Peter Rabbit had a fly upon his nose.

And he swished it and he swashed it,

And the fly flew away.

May be photocopied for classroom use. ©2018 by Irene C. Fountas and Gay Su Pinnell from *Sing a Song of Poetry, Grade 1*. Portsmouth, NH: Heinemann.

**SUGGESTION:** Recite this poem to the tune of "The Battle Hymn of the Republic." Add some rhythm instruments or invite a few children to repeatedly say *swish swash* while the others read.

fold here

# The Little Plant

*by Kate L. Brown*

In the heart of a seed,
Buried deep, so deep,
A dear little plant
Lay fast asleep.

"Wake!" said the sunshine,
"And creep to the light."
"Wake!" said the voice
Of the raindrops bright.

The little plant heard,
And it rose to see
What the wonderful
Outside world might be.

May be photocopied for classroom use. ©2018 by Irene C. Fountas and Gay Su Pinnell from *Sing a Song of Poetry, Grade 1*. Portsmouth, NH: Heinemann.

fold here

**SUGGESTION:** Have the class narrate the poem while one child plays the sunshine and another plays the raindrops. Several children can scrunch down like seeds and slowly "grow" to stretch as high as they can.

# Little Pup, Little Pup

Little pup, little pup,

What do you say?

"Woof, woof, woof!

Let's go and play."


Kitty cat, kitty cat,

How about you?

"Meow, meow, meow!

And I purr, too."


Pretty bird, pretty bird,

Have you a song?

"Tweet, tweet, tweet!

The whole day long."

*continued*

May be photocopied for classroom use. ©2018 by Irene C. Fountas and Gay Su Pinnell from *Sing a Song of Poetry, Grade 1*. Portsmouth, NH: Heinemann.

Jersey cow, jersey cow,

What do you do?

"Moo, moo, moo!

And give milk, too."


Little lamb, little lamb,

What do you say?

"Baa, baa, baa!

Can Mary play?"

May be photocopied for classroom use. ©2018 by Irene C. Fountas and Gay Su Pinnell from *Sing a Song of Poetry, Grade 1*. Portsmouth, NH: Heinemann.

**SUGGESTION:** Once children know the poem, they will enjoy playing this game: one child recites the rhymed question and chooses a classmate to answer it. This person chooses someone to ask the next question. Ten children can play the game each time. Or, add the letter *-s* to all the animal names. Then have small groups of children be the animals and answer in chorus. You can connect the poem to "Mary Had a Little Lamb" (also in this volume).

# Little Raindrops

*by Jane E. Browne*

Oh, where do you come from,

You little drops of rain,

Pitter patter, pitter patter,

Down the windowpane?


They won't let me walk,

And they won't let me play,

And they won't let me go

Out of doors at all today.

ADDITIONAL VERSES:

Tell me, little raindrops,
Is that the way you play,
Pitter patter, pitter patter,
All the rainy day?

They say I'm very naughty,
I have nothing else to do,
But sit here at the window,
I would like to play with you.

The little raindrops cannot speak,
But "pitter, pitter, pat"
Means "We can play on this side,
Why can't you play on that?"

May be photocopied for classroom use. ©2018 by Irene C. Fountas and Gay Su Pinnell from *Sing a Song of Poetry, Grade 1*. Portsmouth, NH: Heinemann.

**SUGGESTION:** Invite children to talk about rain and how it feels. They can also say the words *pitter, patter* and talk about how these words are included in the poem because they sound like rain. It might be nice to place a small version of this poem on a window of the classroom, especially on a rainy day.

fold here

# Little Robin Redbreast

Little robin redbreast,

Sat upon a rail.

Niddle-noodle went his head,

Wibble-wobble went his tail.

ACTIONS:

Little robin redbreast,

Sat upon a rail. [*hold up thumb and little finger and curl down rest of fingers*]

Niddle-nooodle went his head, [*wiggle thumb*]

Wibble-wobble went his tail. [*wiggle little finger*]

May be photocopied for classroom use. ©2018 by Irene C. Fountas and Gay Su Pinnell from *Sing a Song of Poetry, Grade 1*. Portsmouth, NH: Heinemann.

fold here

**SUGGESTION:** This poem is full of imagery. If there is an opportunity, have children observe birds that are perched on trees or telephone lines. Consider also setting up a bird feeder outside a classroom window, and then place the poem by the window. Children can also illustrate the poem with pictures of robins.

# Little Sally Waters

Little Sally Waters, sitting in the sun,

Crying and weeping, lonesome little one.

Rise, Sally, rise;

Wipe off your eyes;

Fly to the east, Sally, fly to the west,

Fly to the one you like the very best.

May be photocopied for classroom use. ©2018 by Irene C. Fountas and Gay Su Pinnell from *Sing a Song of Poetry, Grade 1*. Portsmouth, NH: Heinemann.

fold here

**SUGGESTION:** Assign someone to play Sally [or Wally]. This child sits in the center of the circle and acts out the words *crying* and *weeping* as the other children sing. On cue, Sally [Wally] rises, flies to the east, and then flies to the west. The player she goes to on the last line becomes the next Sally [Wally], and the game goes on until everyone has had a turn.

# Little Silver Airplane

Little silver airplane

Up in the sky,

Where are you going to

Flying so high?

Over the mountains

Over the sea

Little silver airplane

Please take me.

May be photocopied for classroom use. ©2018 by Irene C. Fountas and Gay Su Pinnell from *Sing a Song of Poetry, Grade 1*. Portsmouth, NH: Heinemann.

**SUGGESTION:** Invite children to talk about watching from the ground while airplanes fly in the sky. Where do they think the airplanes go? Who do they think fly the airplanes? If children have flown in an airplane, ask them to describe what it's like looking out an airplane window from the sky.

# Looby-loo

Here we dance, looby-loo,

Here we dance, looby-light,

Here we dance, looby-loo,

All on a Saturday night.


I put my right hand in,

I put my right hand out,

I give my hand a shake, shake, shake,

And turn myself about. Oh,


Here we dance, looby-loo,

Here we dance, looby-light,

Here we dance, looby-loo,

All on a Saturday night.

May be photocopied for classroom use. ©2018 by Irene C. Fountas and Gay Su Pinnell from *Sing a Song of Poetry, Grade 1*. Portsmouth, NH: Heinemann.

**SUGGESTION:** Use the song to play a game; have children join hands and skip in a circle in the direction you indicate, stop and enact the motions described in the second verse, and then skip around in the opposite direction. Let children invent their own actions for the second verse: e.g., *left hand in, right foot in, left elbow in,* and so forth.

fold here

# The Man in the Moon

The man in the moon

Looked out of the moon,

His sides they shook with mirth.

"It's time for all

Children to crawl

Into their beds on Earth."

May be photocopied for classroom use. ©2018 by Irene C. Fountas and Gay Su Pinnell from *Sing a Song of Poetry, Grade 1*. Portsmouth, NH: Heinemann.

VARIATION:

The man in the moon
Came down too soon,
And asked his way to Norwich;
He went by the south
And burned his mouth
While supping on plum porridge.

**SUGGESTION:** You may want to explain that *shook with mirth* means "laughing." Children can laugh and feel their sides shake with mirth. Children are sometimes curious about words such as *porridge*, which can be equated to oatmeal. Ask them to think what *supping* might mean; they will connect it to supper.

# Mary Ann, Mary Ann

Mary Ann, Mary Ann,

Make the porridge in a pan.

Make it thick, make it thin,

Make it any way you can.

May be photocopied for classroom use. ©2018 by Irene C. Fountas and Gay Su Pinnell from *Sing a Song of Poetry, Grade 1*. Portsmouth, NH: Heinemann.

**SUGGESTION:** Substitute different names that include *Ann* such as *Betty Ann, Peggy Ann,* or *Carol Ann.* Invite children to guess what *porridge* is. As they practice, have them recite the verse faster and faster.

fold here

# Mary Had a Little Lamb

Mary had a little lamb,
Little lamb, little lamb.
Mary had a little lamb,
Its fleece was white as snow.

It followed her to school one day,
School one day, school one day.
It followed her to school one day,
Which was against the rule.

It made the children laugh and play,
Laugh and play, laugh and play.
It made the children laugh and play
To see a lamb at school.

May be photocopied for classroom use. ©2018 by Irene C. Fountas and Gay Su Pinnell from *Sing a Song of Poetry, Grade 1*. Portsmouth, NH: Heinemann.

ADDITIONAL VERSES:

And so the teacher turned it out,
Turned it out, turned it out,
And so the teacher turned it out,
But still it lingered near.

What makes the lamb love Mary so,
Mary so, Mary so?
What makes the lamb love Mary so?
The eager children cry.

Why, Mary loves the lamb, you know,
Lamb, you know, lamb, you know,
Why, Mary loves the lamb, you know,
The teacher did reply.

fold here

**SUGGESTION:** Explain to children that *to turn out* means "to remove"; the teacher removed the lamb from school. Link this poem with Sarah Hale's picture book *Mary Had a Little Lamb* (1990), photo-illustrated by Bruce McMillan (this will be especially helpful for English language learners).

# Mary Wore Her Red Dress

Mary wore her red dress, red dress, red dress.

Mary wore her red dress

All day long.

Mary wore her red hat, red hat, red hat.

Mary wore her red hat

All day long.

Mary wore her red shoes, red shoes, red shoes.

Mary wore her red shoes

All day long.

Mary wore her red gloves, red gloves, red gloves.

Mary wore her red gloves

All day long.

Mary was a red bird, red bird, red bird.

Mary was a red bird

All day long!

May be photocopied for classroom use. ©2018 by Irene C. Fountas and Gay Su Pinnell from *Sing a Song of Poetry, Grade 1*. Portsmouth, NH: Heinemann.

**SUGGESTION:** This is an old Texas folksong. Eliminate the last verse and make it a poem about different children wearing different-color clothes. Children enjoy substituting their own names and color choices. You may want to pair this poem with the story of Kate Bear's birthday party in Merle Peek's picture book *Mary Wore Her Red Dress and Henry Wore His Green Sneakers* (1985).

fold here

# Mary's Canary

Mary had a pretty bird,

Feathers bright and yellow,

Slender legs—upon my word

He was a pretty fellow.


The sweetest note he always sung,

Which much delighted Mary.

She often, where the cage was hung,

Sat hearing her canary.

May be photocopied for classroom use. ©2018 by Irene C. Fountas and Gay Su Pinnell from *Sing a Song of Poetry, Grade 1*. Portsmouth, NH: Heinemann.

**SUGGESTION:** Ask two children to act out or pantomime this verse as the class recites it together. As an alternative, consider dividing the class and allowing one group to become audible canaries as background for the second verse. And then repeat, giving the other group a chance to do their birdcalls. This is also a fun poem to revisit when children are working to recognize rhymes and/or identifying one-, two-, and three-syllable words.

# Merrily We Roll Along

Merrily we roll along,

Roll along, roll along.

Merrily we roll along,

O'er the deep blue sea.

May be photocopied for classroom use. ©2018 by Irene C. Fountas and Gay Su Pinnell from *Sing a Song of Poetry, Grade 1*. Portsmouth, NH: Heinemann.

fold here

**SUGGESTION**: Invite children to say the rhyme in unison or as a round. Explain that *o'er* is a contraction for the word *over* that people sometimes use in poems. When you finish reading the poem, invite children to name all the ways they might roll across the sea: e.g., canoe, sailboat, submarine, kayak, and speed boat.

# Monday Morning

This is the way we wash our clothes,

Wash our clothes, wash our clothes,

This is the way we wash our clothes

All on a Monday morning.


This is the way we hang them up,

Hang them up, hang them up,

This is the way we hang them up

All on a Monday morning.


This is the way we fold our clothes,

Fold our clothes, fold our clothes,

This is the way we fold our clothes

All on a Monday morning.

May be photocopied for classroom use. ©2018 by Irene C. Fountas and Gay Su Pinnell from *Sing a Song of Poetry, Grade 1.* Portsmouth, NH: Heinemann.

fold here

**SUGGESTION:** Create new *This is the way* verses with the same structure. Substitute the names of other days of the week.

# Moon, Moon

Moon, moon,

Silvery spoon,

Floating still

On a night in June.


Moon, moon,

Back too soon,

White and pale

In the afternoon.

May be photocopied for classroom use. ©2018 by Irene C. Fountas and Gay Su Pinnell from *Sing a Song of Poetry, Grade 1*. Portsmouth, NH: Heinemann.

**SUGGESTION:** Ask children if they have ever seen the moon in the sky during the day. Then discuss the many different ways the moon looks during the day and at night.

fold here

# The Moon Shines Bright

The moon shines bright,

The stars give a light.

You may play at any game

At ten o'clock at night.

May be photocopied for classroom use. ©2018 by Irene C. Fountas and Gay Su Pinnell from *Sing a Song of Poetry, Grade 1*. Portsmouth, NH: Heinemann.

fold here

**SUGGESTION:** Use this poem right before summer vacation. Children may remember how the days are very long around this time of year. Prompt them to remember this poem as they are playing late.

# The More We Get Together

Oh, the more we get together,

Together, together,

Oh, the more we get together,

The happier we'll be.


For your friends are my friends,

And my friends are your friends.

Oh, the more we get together,

The happier we'll be!

May be photocopied for classroom use. ©2018 by Irene C. Fountas and Gay Su Pinnell from *Sing a Song of Poetry, Grade 1*. Portsmouth, NH: Heinemann.

**SUGGESTION:** The repetition in this song will make it enjoyable to sing. It may be interesting for children to examine the first two sentences of the second verse. They can discuss how they sound almost alike and have the same words but the meaning is slightly changed.

fold here

# Mouse in a Hole

A mouse lived in a little hole,

Lived quietly in a little hole.

When all was quiet, as quiet as can be . . .

OUT POPPED HE!

May be photocopied for classroom use. ©2018 by Irene C. Fountas and Gay Su Pinnell from *Sing a Song of Poetry, Grade 1*. Portsmouth, NH: Heinemann.

fold here    **SUGGESTION:** Invite children to read the third line very softly and then pop up and shout the last line.

# My Apple

Look at my apple,

It is nice and round.

It fell from a tree,

Down to the ground.

Come, let me share my apple, please do!

My mother can cut it half in two—

One half for me

And one half for you.

ACTIONS:

Look at my apple,

It is nice and round. [*cup hands*]

It fell from a tree,

Down to the ground. [*move fingers in a downward motion*]

Come, let me share my apple, please do! [*beckoning motion*]

My mother can cut it half in two— [*slicing motion*]

One half for me

And one half for you. [*hold out two hands, sharing halves*]

**SUGGESTION:** Invite children to talk about what *sharing* and *half* mean in the poem. What would they do if there were three friends? (*My mother can cut it into three—one for each of you and one for me.*)

fold here

May be photocopied for classroom use. ©2018 by Irene C. Fountas and Gay Su Pinnell from *Sing a Song of Poetry, Grade 1.* Portsmouth, NH: Heinemann.

# My Aunt Jane

My Aunt Jane,

She came from France,

To teach to me the polka dance;

First the heel,

And then the toe,

That's the way

The dance should go.

May be photocopied for classroom use. ©2018 by Irene C. Fountas and Gay Su Pinnell from *Sing a Song of Poetry, Grade 1.* Portsmouth, NH: Heinemann.

**SUGGESTION:** Children enjoy moving from one leg to another and, while standing on one leg, tapping heel and toe of the other. This dance will provide quick exercise; use this poem after the class has been sitting for a long period of time.

# My Big Balloon

I can make a big balloon,

Watch me while I blow.

Small at first then bigger,

Watch it grow and grow.


Do you think it's big enough?

Maybe I should stop.

For if I blow much longer,

My balloon will surely POP!

May be photocopied for classroom use. ©2018 by Irene C. Fountas and Gay Su Pinnell from *Sing a Song of Poetry, Grade 1*. Portsmouth, NH: Heinemann.

**SUGGESTION:** Blow up a balloon while children recite the words. Invite them to shout *POP!* on the last line when the balloon is nearly full. Print the words to the poem on a poetry chart for children to illustrate. Assign one child to write *POP!* on the chart in capital letters.

# My Bike

One wheel, two wheels, on the ground,

My feet make the pedals go 'round and 'round.

The handlebars help me steer so straight,

Down the sidewalk and through the gate.

ACTIONS:

One wheel, two wheels, on the ground, [*make circle with arms*]

My feet make the pedals go 'round and 'round. [*lift feet and pretend to pedal bike*]

The handlebars help me steer so straight, [*pretend to steer*]

Down the sidewalk and through the gate. [*shade eyes as if looking at something in the distance*]

May be photocopied for classroom use. ©2018 by Irene C. Fountas and Gay Su Pinnell from *Sing a Song of Poetry, Grade 1*. Portsmouth, NH: Heinemann.

fold here

**SUGGESTION:** Have children act out the poem as shown above. Give them a reproduced copy, and invite them to illustrate it with a bike—coloring and decorating it as they like.

# My Bonnie Lies over the Ocean

My Bonnie lies over the ocean,
My Bonnie lies over the sea.
My Bonnie lies over the ocean,
Please bring back my Bonnie to me.

*Chorus*
Bring back, bring back,
Oh, bring back my Bonnie to me, to me.
Bring back, bring back,
Oh, bring back my Bonnie to me.

Oh, blow ye winds over the ocean,
And blow ye winds over the sea.
Oh, blow ye winds over the ocean,
And bring back my Bonnie to me.

*Chorus*

The winds have blown over the ocean,
The winds have blown over the sea.
The winds have blown over the ocean,
And brought back my Bonnie to me.

*Chorus*

May be photocopied for classroom use. ©2018 by Irene C. Fountas and Gay Su Pinnell from *Sing a Song of Poetry, Grade 1*. Portsmouth, NH: Heinemann.

fold here

**SUGGESTION:** Children may want to talk about *Bonnie* as a girl's name, but teach them that it also means "pretty" and might be something to call someone you like—a girl or a boy. (Originally, the song was about Bonnie Prince Charlie.)

# My Favorite Toys

I have a lot of favorite toys.
I cannot choose just one.
I need to keep them all around
For different kinds of fun.

A book, a doll,
A drum, a ball,
And, of course, my teddy bear.
A wagon, a bike,
And finally I like
The jack-in-the-box sitting there.

As you can see, I need them all
For work and play and rest.
When you go home to find your toys,
Which ones do you like best?

May be photocopied for classroom use. ©2018 by Irene C. Fountas and Gay Su Pinnell from *Sing a Song of Poetry, Grade 1*. Portsmouth, NH: Heinemann.

fold here

**SUGGESTION:** Use interactive writing to make a chart or class book about toys. ("Rayshawn's favorite toy is _____.")
They will be adding more modern toys to the list. Each child can make an illustration to glue on the chart or in the book.

# My Hat, It Has Three Corners

My hat, it has three corners,

Three corners has my hat;

And had it not three corners,

It would not be my hat.

May be photocopied for classroom use. ©2018 by Irene C. Fountas and Gay Su Pinnell from *Sing a Song of Poetry, Grade 1*. Portsmouth, NH: Heinemann.

ACTIONS:

My hat, it has three corners [*point to self*]

Three corners has my hat; [*point to head*]

And had it not three corners, [*hold up three fingers*]

It would not be my hat. [*shake head*]

fold here

**SUGGESTION:** This poem was originally created to teach children how to act out words instead of saying them: e.g., the word *hat*. After children are familiar with the poem, put it in a pocket chart with individual word cards. Create a name card for each child in the class, and place them in a column next to the displayed poem. Switch out the *my* word cards with a child's name, and ask the class to read the poem. Then invite the child whose name was added to the poem to pick a new classmate's name. Reread the poem, each time with a new child's name, until the class can read and act it out quickly.

# My Little Toys

Smiling girls, rosy boys,

Come and buy my little toys;

Monkeys made of gingerbread,

And sugar horses painted red.

May be photocopied for classroom use. ©2018 by Irene C. Fountas and Gay Su Pinnell from *Sing a Song of Poetry, Grade 1*. Portsmouth, NH: Heinemann.

**SUGGESTION:** Have children clap, snap, or whisper the rhyming words. Invite them to illustrate the poem, especially the fun, nonsensical images in the last two lines. Ask children what other silly images they might substitute here and guide their creation of rhyming lines: e.g., *Dolls with braided, rainbow hairdos / And edible cars painted blue.* Afterwards, have children draw the new images accordingly.

# My Love for You

I know you little,

I love you lots;

My love for you

Would fill ten pots,

Fifteen buckets,

Sixteen cans,

Three teacups,

And four dishpans.

May be photocopied for classroom use. ©2018 by Irene C. Fountas and Gay Su Pinnell from *Sing a Song of Poetry, Grade 1.* Portsmouth, NH: Heinemann.

**SUGGESTION:** Invite children to substitute other number words or objects to create new verses of this poem.

fold here

# Night, Knight

"Night, night,"

Said one knight

To the other knight

The other night.

"Night, night, Knight."

May be photocopied for classroom use. ©2018 by Irene C. Fountas and Gay Su Pinnell from *Sing a Song of Poetry, Grade 1*. Portsmouth, NH: Heinemann.

fold here

**SUGGESTION:** Children may know what a *knight* is from games or television. If not, explain the word *knight* and ask them to compare it with *night*. Invite them to talk about what makes the tongue twister funny.

# Nut Tree

I had a little nut tree,

Nothing would it bear,

But a silver nutmeg

And a golden pear.


The king of Spain's daughter

Came to visit me,

And all for the sake

Of my little nut tree.


I skipped over water,

I danced over sea,

And all the birds

Couldn't catch me.

May be photocopied for classroom use. ©2018 by Irene C. Fountas and Gay Su Pinnell from *Sing a Song of Poetry, Grade 1*. Portsmouth, NH: Heinemann.

fold here

**SUGGESTION:** While teaching children this nursery song, play a recorded version with music to help enhance the words. Talk about why the images of a *silver nutmeg* and *golden pear* are magical. Ask children what other images they like from this poem and why.

# Oats, Peas, Beans

Oats, peas, beans, and barley grow,

Oats, peas, beans, and barley grow,

Do you or I or anyone know

How oats, peas, beans, and barley grow?


First the farmer sows his seeds,

Then he stands and takes his ease,

Stamps his feet, and claps his hands,

And turns around to view the land.


Waiting for a partner,

Waiting for a partner,

Open the ring and take one in,

And then we'll dance and gaily sing.

May be photocopied for classroom use. ©2018 by Irene C. Fountas and Gay Su Pinnell from *Sing a Song of Poetry, Grade 1*. Portsmouth, NH: Heinemann.

fold here

**SUGGESTION:** Have one child play the part of the farmer and stand in the center of a circle. Ask the rest of the class to join hands and skip left as they sing. Invite the farmer to act out the second verse and then choose a partner during the third verse while the class continues to skip around. The partner or another child now becomes the farmer, and the song is repeated. John Langstaff's CD *Songs for Singing Children* (1996) includes a great rendition of this old song.

# Old Dan Tucker

Old Dan Tucker went to town

Riding a goat and leading a hound.

The hound gave a yelp and the goat gave a jump

And old Dan Tucker landed on a stump.

May be photocopied for classroom use. ©2018 by Irene C. Fountas and Gay Su Pinnell from *Sing a Song of Poetry, Grade 1*. Portsmouth, NH: Heinemann.

**SUGGESTION**: Children can talk about what riding a goat would be like and why it would be so hard to do. After they know the poem, invite them to quickly locate words that end with *-mp*.

fold here

# The Old Gray Cat

The old gray cat is sleeping, sleeping, sleeping,

The old gray cat is sleeping in the house.


The little mice are creeping, creeping, creeping,

The little mice are creeping through the house.


The old gray cat is waking, waking, waking,

The old gray cat is waking in the house.


The old gray cat is chasing, chasing, chasing,

The old gray cat is chasing through the house.


All the mice are squealing, squealing, squealing,

All the mice are squealing through the house.

May be photocopied for classroom use. ©2018 by Irene C. Fountas and Gay Su Pinnell from *Sing a Song of Poetry, Grade 1*. Portsmouth, NH: Heinemann.

fold here

**SUGGESTION:** This song is fun for children to act out. It also is a good base for a five-page book that they can illustrate and use for shared reading. Have children locate words with *-ing* at the end. Then point out the different uses of the words *in* and *through*.

# The Old Woman

The old woman must stand at the tub, tub, tub,

The dirty clothes to rub, rub, rub.

But when they are clean and fit to be seen,

She'll dress like a lady and dance on the green.

May be photocopied for classroom use. ©2018 by Irene C. Fountas and Gay Su Pinnell from *Sing a Song of Poetry, Grade 1*. Portsmouth, NH: Heinemann.

**SUGGESTION:** Ask children what they think *the green* might be (a grassy area, a park, a place where people meet to talk or dance). The act of rubbing dirty clothes clean is another archaic concept that may require definition and context.

fold here

# On Saturday Night

On Saturday night I lost my wife,

And where do you think I found her?

Up in the moon, singing a tune,

And all the stars around her.

May be photocopied for classroom use. ©2018 by Irene C. Fountas and Gay Su Pinnell from *Sing a Song of Poetry, Grade 1*. Portsmouth, NH: Heinemann.

fold here

**SUGGESTION:** Invite children to substitute other family words for *wife*: e.g., *sister, mother, father,* or *brother*. If they pick a family word with a new gender, ask children what other word needs to change in the poem.

# On Top of Spaghetti

On top of spaghetti,

All covered with cheese,

I lost my last meatball,

When somebody sneezed.


It rolled off the table

And onto the floor

And then my poor meatball

Rolled out of the door.


So, if you eat spaghetti,

All covered with cheese,

Hold on to your meatballs,

And don't ever sneeze.

May be photocopied for classroom use. ©2018 by Irene C. Fountas and Gay Su Pinnell from *Sing a Song of Poetry, Grade 1*. Portsmouth, NH: Heinemann.

**SUGGESTION:** Children will love singing this nonsense song to the tune of "On Top of Old Smokey." Invite them to play with the poem by brainstorming other favorite food dishes: e.g., *On top of ice cream, / All covered in syrup, / I lost my last cherry, / When loudly I hiccuped.*

fold here

# One Finger, One Thumb, Keep Moving

One finger, one thumb, keep moving,

One finger, one thumb, keep moving,

One finger, one thumb, keep moving,

We'll all be merry and bright.


One finger, one thumb, one arm, keep moving,

One finger, one thumb, one arm, keep moving,

One finger, one thumb, one arm, keep moving,

We'll all be merry and bright.


One finger, one thumb, one arm, one leg, keep moving,

One finger, one thumb, one arm, one leg, keep moving,

One finger, one thumb, one arm, one leg, keep moving,

We'll all be merry and bright.


ADDITIONAL VERSES:

One finger, one thumb, one arm, one leg, one nod of the head, keep moving . . . .

One finger, one thumb, one arm, one leg, one nod of the head, stand up, sit down, keep moving . . .

One finger, one thumb, one arm, one leg, one nod of the head, stand up, sit down, turn around, keep moving . . .

fold here

**SUGGESTION:** This poem gives children a chance to move around and stretch as they say the words and perform the actions, adding one additional body part with each new verse. You can find the melody on the Internet.

May be photocopied for classroom use. ©2018 by Irene C. Fountas and Gay Su Pinnell from *Sing a Song of Poetry, Grade 1.* Portsmouth, NH: Heinemann.

# One for the Money

One for the money,

Two for the show,

Three to make ready,

And four to go!

May be photocopied for classroom use. ©2018 by Irene C. Fountas and Gay Su Pinnell from *Sing a Song of Poetry, Grade 1*. Portsmouth, NH: Heinemann.

**SUGGESTION:** Children can hold up the right number of fingers for the lines of the poem. Use this poem as children are getting ready to line up and leave at the end of the day.

fold here

# One for Sorrow

One for sorrow,

Two for joy,

Three for a girl,

Four for a boy,

Five for silver,

Six for gold,

Seven for a secret

Never to be told.

May be photocopied for classroom use. ©2018 by Irene C. Fountas and Gay Su Pinnell from *Sing a Song of Poetry, Grade 1*. Portsmouth, NH: Heinemann.

**SUGGESTION:** Have children hold up the correct number of fingers on each line. Create new verses with the same structure.

# One Man Went to Mow

One man went to mow,

Went to mow a meadow.

One man and his dog

Went to mow a meadow.


Two men went to mow,

Went to mow a meadow.

Two men, one man and his dog

Went to mow a meadow.


Three men went to mow,

Went to mow a meadow.

Three men, two men, one man and his dog

Went to mow a meadow.

May be photocopied for classroom use. ©2018 by Irene C. Fountas and Gay Su Pinnell from *Sing a Song of Poetry, Grade 1*. Portsmouth, NH: Heinemann.

**SUGGESTION:** How do you mow a meadow? City children and English language learners may need to see a picture or photograph of a meadow to help make the concept clear. Continue the rhyme to ten, increasing the number of men with each stanza.

fold here

# One Misty, Moisty Morning

One misty, moisty morning

When cloudy was the weather,

There I met an old man

Clothed all in leather.


He began to compliment

And I began to grin,

"How do you do?"

And "How do you do?"

And "How do you do?" again!

May be photocopied for classroom use. ©2018 by Irene C. Fountas and Gay Su Pinnell from *Sing a Song of Poetry, Grade 1*. Portsmouth, NH: Heinemann.

fold here   **SUGGESTION:** The repeating of /s/ in the first line sets a damp, foggy mood. Invite pairs of children to act out the rhyme—one as the child, one as the old man—by taking off their imaginary hats, bowing, and saying *How do you do?*

# One, Two, How Do You Do?

One, two,
How do you do?
One, two, three,
Clap with me.
One, two, three, four,
Jump on the floor.
One, two, three, four, five,
Look bright and alive.
One, two, three, four, five, six,
Your shoe we'll have to fix.
One, two, three, four, five, six, seven,
Can we make it to eleven?
One, two, three, four, five, six, seven, eight,
Draw a circle on a big round plate.
One, two, three, four, five, six, seven, eight, nine,
Get ready, it's time to stand in line.
One, two, three, four, five, six, seven, eight, nine, ten,
Let's go back and start all over again.

May be photocopied for classroom use. ©2018 by Irene C. Fountas and Gay Su Pinnell from *Sing a Song of Poetry, Grade 1*. Portsmouth, NH: Heinemann.

**SUGGESTION:** Children enjoy acting this poem out; it's especially fun for children to pair up with a partner and make up actions for the noncounting lines: e.g., bow to each other while reciting *How do you do?*

fold here

# One, Two, Three, Four, Five

One, two, three, four, five,

Once I caught a fish alive.

Six, seven, eight, nine, ten,

Then I let him go again.

Why did you let him go?

Because he bit my finger so.

Which finger did he bite?

This little finger on the right.

May be photocopied for classroom use. ©2018 by Irene C. Fountas and Gay Su Pinnell from *Sing a Song of Poetry, Grade 1*. Portsmouth, NH: Heinemann.

fold here

**SUGGESTION:** Invite children to act out this poem while reciting it: e.g., pretending to catch a fish. Asking children to create their own motions will help them remember the words.

# Out

Out goes the rat,

Out goes the cat,

Out goes the lady

With the big green hat.

Y – O – U spells you,

O – U – T spells out!

May be photocopied for classroom use. ©2018 by Irene C. Fountas and Gay Su Pinnell from *Sing a Song of Poetry, Grade 1.* Portsmouth, NH: Heinemann.

fold here

**SUGGESTION:** This poem may be recited as a jump-rope rhyme. Alternatively, invite children to recite it while playing a counting-out circle game. Assign one child to be "it." Ask the rest of the class to form a circle around the child who is "it." Instruct the child in the center to point to ten students, one at a time, while saying *Y–O–U spells you, O–U–T spells out!* The child who "it" points to on the word *out* is out and trades places with "it" by going to the center to count someone else out.

# Papa's Glasses

These are Papa's glasses.

This is Papa's hat.

This is how he folds his hands

And puts them in his lap.

ACTIONS:

These are Papa's glasses. [*make glasses with fingers*]

This is Papa's hat. [*tap head*]

This is how he folds his hands [*fold hands*]

And puts them in his lap. [*place hands in lap*]

May be photocopied for classroom use. ©2018 by Irene C. Fountas and Gay Su Pinnell from *Sing a Song of Poetry, Grade 1*. Portsmouth, NH: Heinemann.

fold here

**SUGGESTION:** Have children complete the actions along with the poem. Create new verses about Nana's or Grandma's glasses. Alternatively, invite children to substitute each other's names for *Papa* and have the named child act out the poem while others say it.

# Peanut Butter and Jelly

First you take the peanuts,

And you dig 'em, you dig 'em,

Dig 'em, dig 'em, dig 'em.

Then you crush 'em, you crush 'em,

Crush 'em, crush 'em, crush 'em.

Then you spread 'em, you spread 'em,

Spread 'em, spread 'em, spread 'em.

For your peanut, peanut butter and jelly,

Peanut, peanut butter and jelly.

ADDITIONAL VERSES:

Then you take the berries,

And you pick 'em, you pick 'em,

Pick 'em, pick 'em, pick 'em.

Then you smash 'em, you smash 'em,

Smash 'em, smash 'em, smash 'em.

Then you smooth 'em, you smooth 'em,

Smooth 'em, smooth 'em, smooth 'em.

For your peanut, peanut butter and jelly,

Peanut, peanut butter and jelly.

Then you take the sandwich,

And you bite it, you bite it,

Bite it, bite it, bite it.

Then you chew it, you chew it,

Chew it, chew it, chew it.

Then you swallow it, you swallow it,

Swallow it, swallow it, swallow it.

'Cause it's peanut, peanut butter and jelly,

Peanut, peanut butter and jelly.

**SUGGESTION:** There are several different versions of this popular poem; try to compare them as a class. If you are working with a written version, children may be curious about the use of apostrophes in *'em* and *'cause*. This visual will help them understand that apostrophes sometimes stand for letters that have been left out of words.

fold here

May be photocopied for classroom use. ©2018 by Irene C. Fountas and Gay Su Pinnell from *Sing a Song of Poetry, Grade 1*. Portsmouth, NH: Heinemann.

# Peter Piper

Peter Piper picked a peck of pickled peppers;

A peck of pickled peppers Peter Piper picked.

If Peter Piper picked a peck of pickled peppers,

Where's the peck of pickled peppers Peter Piper picked?

May be photocopied for classroom use. ©2018 by Irene C. Fountas and Gay Su Pinnell from *Sing a Song of Poetry, Grade 1*. Portsmouth, NH: Heinemann.

fold here

**SUGGESTION:** This tongue twister can be read and recited slowly at first and then faster and faster. Children might need help with the concept of a *peck of pickled peppers*. Ask them what foods their families buy in large quantities.

# Polly, Put the Kettle On

Polly, put the kettle on,

Polly, put the kettle on,

Polly, put the kettle on,

We'll all have tea.


Sukey, take it off again,

Sukey, take it off again,

Sukey, take it off again,

They've all gone home.

May be photocopied for classroom use. ©2018 by Irene C. Fountas and Gay Su Pinnell from *Sing a Song of Poetry, Grade 1*. Portsmouth, NH: Heinemann.

**SUGGESTION:** Have children sing or chant the text with a partner, clapping each other's palms and then their own to the beat. Let them substitute their own names.

fold here

# Polly Wolly Doodle

Oh, I went down South
For to see my Sal
Sing Polly wolly doodle all the day
My Sal, she is
A spunky gal
Sing Polly wolly doodle all the day

*Chorus*
Fare thee well, fare thee well
Fare thee well my fairy fay
For I'm going to Lou'siana
For to see my Susyanna
Sing Polly wolly doodle all the day

ADDITIONAL VERSES:

Behind the barn,
Down on my knees
Sing Polly wolly doodle all the day
I thought I heard
A chicken sneeze
Sing Polly wolly doodle all the day

*Chorus*

He sneezed so hard
With the whooping cough
Sing Polly wolly doodle all the day
He sneezed his head
And the tail right off
Sing Polly wolly doodle all the day

Oh, a grasshopper sittin'
On a railroad track
Sing Polly wolly doodle all the day
A-pickin' his teeth
With a carpet tack
Sing Polly wolly doodle all the day.

*Chorus*

Oh, I went to bed
But it wasn't any use
Sing Polly wolly doodle all the day
My feet stuck out
Like a chicken roost
Sing Polly wolly doodle all the day

*Chorus*

May be photocopied for classroom use. ©2018 by Irene C. Fountas and Gay Su Pinnell from *Sing a Song of Poetry, Grade 1*. Portsmouth, NH: Heinemann.

fold here

**SUGGESTION:** Children will enjoy singing this traditional song. As they learn verses, look at the funny aspects of the song. Use judgment about how many verses to teach children at once; continue to add verses throughout the year as they learn the song.

# Pop! Goes the Weasel

All around the mulberry bush,

The monkey chased the weasel,

The monkey thought t'was all in fun,

Pop! goes the weasel.


A penny for a spool of thread,

A penny for a needle,

That's the way the money goes,

Pop! goes the weasel.


Rufus has the whooping cough,

Poor Sally has the measles,

That's the way the doctor goes,

Pop! goes the weasel.

May be photocopied for classroom use. ©2018 by Irene C. Fountas and Gay Su Pinnell from *Sing a Song of Poetry, Grade 1*. Portsmouth, NH: Heinemann.

**SUGGESTION:** Children will enjoy singing the words and jumping up to shout *Pop!* Some may need an explanation of the word *weasel*; you may also need to define the archaic use of *t'was* Play a recording of a sung version, or invite children to play the tune on homemade kazoos (tape or rubber-band a square of waxed paper around one end of a paper tube, have children place their mouths over the other end of the tube, and then hum).

fold here

# Pumpkin Orange

We had a pumpkin orange.

We gave it two big eyes.

We cut around a tiny nose

A funny mouth that smiles.


Now we'll hide behind the hedge

And wait until it's dark.

Then when _____ comes along,

Up we'll jump! "Boo!" we'll shout!


What a surprise!

May be photocopied for classroom use. ©2018 by Irene C. Fountas and Gay Su Pinnell from *Sing a Song of Poetry, Grade 1*. Portsmouth, NH: Heinemann.

**SUGGESTION:** After children have learned the poem, give them time to create the perfect props: orange jack-o'-lanterns attached to tongue depressors or craft sticks to hold up when they shout *Boo!* For variety and suspense, insert different children's names in the poem.

# The Queen of Hearts

The Queen of Hearts

She made some tarts,

All on a summer's day.

The Knave of Hearts

He stole the tarts

And took them clean away.

The King of Hearts

Called for the tarts

Until his voice was sore.

The Knave of Hearts

Brought back the tarts

And said he'd steal no more.

May be photocopied for classroom use. ©2018 by Irene C. Fountas and Gay Su Pinnell from *Sing a Song of Poetry, Grade 1*. Portsmouth, NH: Heinemann.

**SUGGESTION:** Children need to know that *tarts* are "little pies with no top crust usually filled with something sweet," such as jam, custard, or fruit. They also need to know about royalty: kings, queen, knaves, and so forth. Invite children to make paper crowns and other royal props. Then divide the class into four groups and have each group read one stanza of the poem.

fold here

# Ring-a-Ring

*by Kate Greenaway*

Ring-a-ring of little boys.

Ring-a-ring of girls.

All around, all around,

Twists and twirls.


You are merry children;

"Yes, we are."

Where do you come from?

"Not very far."


"We live in the mountain,

We live in the tree;

And I live in the river-bed,

And you won't catch me!"

May be photocopied for classroom use. ©2018 by Irene C. Fountas and Gay Su Pinnell from *Sing a Song of Poetry, Grade 1*. Portsmouth, NH: Heinemann.

**SUGGESTION:** Ask all but one boy to form a circle; invite all but one girl to do the same. Have children *twist and twirl* in place while the one boy and one girl circle around their respective rings. Read the teacher part to the class. When it's time for the *merry children* to recite their lines, have the boys and girls do so in unison. On the last line, invite the single boy and girl to tag a classmate, whose goal is to catch them. The goal of the taggers is to run around the circle and back to the open spot before being caught. Repeat until the poem is familiar and all boys and girls get to be taggers.

# Roosters Crow

Roosters crow in the morn

To tell us to rise,

And he who lies late

Will never be wise.


For early to bed

And early to rise

Is the way to be healthy

And wealthy and wise.

May be photocopied for classroom use. ©2018 by Irene C. Fountas and Gay Su Pinnell from *Sing a Song of Poetry, Grade 1*. Portsmouth, NH: Heinemann.

fold here

**SUGGESTION:** This poem presents an archaic concept that children may not know; people used to depend on the sound of a rooster's crow to wake them up at dawn. Compare a rooster's crow to an alarm clock. Discuss why it is important to get enough sleep.

# 'Round and 'Round

'Round and 'round the garden

Went the teddy bear;

One step,

Two steps,

And he's almost there.


'Round and 'round the haystack

Went the little mouse;

One step,

Two steps,

In his little house.

May be photocopied for classroom use. ©2018 by Irene C. Fountas and Gay Su Pinnell from *Sing a Song of Poetry, Grade 1*. Portsmouth, NH: Heinemann.

fold here

**SUGGESTION:** If your class has a teddy bear, this may be the time he gets to take a spin from child to child while reciting the poem. Alternatively, have children say this poem while lining up to leave the classroom.

# Sam, Sam, the Butcher Man

Sam, Sam, the butcher man,

Washed his face in a frying pan,

Combed his hair with a wagon wheel,

And died with a toothache in his heel.

May be photocopied for classroom use. ©2018 by Irene C. Fountas and Gay Su Pinnell from *Sing a Song of Poetry, Grade 1*. Portsmouth, NH: Heinemann.

**SUGGESTION:** This nonsense poem uses funny images. Invite children to play with humor by substituting other names, occupations, objects, sicknesses, and parts of the body: e.g., *John, John, the fireman, / Washed his hands in a pizza pan, / Combed his hair with a hunk of cheese, / And died with an earache in his knees.*

fold here

# Say and Touch

Say *red* and touch your head.

Say *sky* and touch your eye.

Say *bear* and touch your hair.

Say *hear* and touch your ear.

Say *south* and touch your mouth.

Say *rose* and touch your nose.

Say *in* and touch your chin.

Say *rest* and touch your chest.

Say *farm* and touch your arm.

Say *yummy* and touch your tummy.

Say *bee* and touch your knee.

Say *neat* and touch your feet.

May be photocopied for classroom use. ©2018 by Irene C. Fountas and Gay Su Pinnell from *Sing a Song of Poetry, Grade 1*. Portsmouth, NH: Heinemann.

fold here

**SUGGESTION:** This poem is a little like the classic game Simon Says. Children recite the rhymes as they point to the body part named: e.g., *head, eye, ear*, and so on. After they know the poem, the person who is "it" (the teacher at first) can say a verse that does not rhyme. Instruct children to only follow directions on a rhyme.

# She'll Be Coming 'Round the Mountain

She'll be coming 'round the mountain

When she comes, toot, toot,

She'll be coming 'round the mountain

When she comes, toot, toot,

She'll be coming 'round the mountain,

She'll be coming 'round the mountain,

She'll be coming 'round the mountain

When she comes, toot, toot.

ADDITIONAL VERSES:

She'll be driving six white horses

When she comes, whoa, back,

She'll be driving six white horses

When she comes, whoa, back,

She'll be driving six white horses,

She'll be driving six white horses,

She'll be driving six white horses

When she comes, whoa, back.

And we'll all sing "Welcome"

When she comes, oh, yes,

And we'll all sing "Welcome"

When she comes, oh, yes,

And we'll all sing "Welcome,"

Oh we'll all sing "Welcome,"

And we'll all sing "Welcome"

When she comes, oh, yes.

May be photocopied for classroom use. ©2018 by Irene C. Fountas and Gay Su Pinnell from *Sing a Song of Poetry, Grade 1*. Portsmouth, NH: Heinemann.

SUGGESTION: If you have children in your classroom who speak other languages, invite them to teach classmates how to say *welcome* or *hello* in those languages. Then sing the song again, replacing *Welcome* with a greeting in another language. You can connect this poem with the book *Coming Around the Mountain* adapted by Norma Morris and found in the *Fountas & Pinnell Classroom™ Shared Reading Collection, Grade 1* (2018).

fold here

# Shoo Fly

Shoo fly, don't bother me.

Shoo fly, don't bother me.

Shoo fly, don't bother me.

For I belong to somebody.

May be photocopied for classroom use. ©2018 by Irene C. Fountas and Gay Su Pinnell from *Sing a Song of Poetry, Grade 1*. Portsmouth, NH: Heinemann.

**SUGGESTION:** Extend this exuberant song by sharing Iza Trapani's picture book *Shoo Fly!* (2000), the story of an intrepid mouse who fights a persistent fly. The music and words to all the verses of the song are included on the last page of the book. Seeing the illustrations while hearing the story supports English language learners and gives them a stimulating experience with language.

# Sing a Rainbow

Red and yellow, pink and green,

Orange and purple, and blue,

I can sing a rainbow,

Sing a rainbow,

Sing a rainbow too.

May be photocopied for classroom use. ©2018 by Irene C. Fountas and Gay Su Pinnell from *Sing a Song of Poetry, Grade 1*. Portsmouth, NH: Heinemann.

**SUGGESTION:** After children are familiar with the poem, divide them into seven color groups and invite them to pick out small classroom objects reflecting their group's color. Now have children recite the poem again. When their group's color is called, invite one child from each color group to set his or her object on the floor. Have children repeat the poem until each child's object from each color group is displayed on the floor in the shape of a rainbow. This is a great song. You can find the tune on the Internet.

fold here

# Sing a Song of Sixpence

Sing a song of sixpence,
A pocket full of rye.
Four and twenty blackbirds
Baked in a pie!

When the pie was opened,
The birds began to sing.
Wasn't that a dainty dish
To set before the king?

The king was in the counting-house,
Counting out his money.
The queen was in the parlor,
Eating bread and honey.

The maid was in the garden,
Hanging out the clothes
When down came a blackbird
And snapped off her nose!

May be photocopied for classroom use. ©2018 by Irene C. Fountas and Gay Su Pinnell from *Sing a Song of Poetry, Grade 1*. Portsmouth, NH: Heinemann.

fold here

**SUGGESTION:** Have children sing the song. They can snap fingers or clap on the word *snapped*. Then divide children into four groups, and invite each to practice one stanza to perform for the rest of the class using props made from classroom materials.

# Sing, Sing

Sing, sing,

What shall I sing?

That cat's run away

With the pudding string!


Do, do,

What shall I do?

The cat's run away

With the pudding, too.

May be photocopied for classroom use. ©2018 by Irene C. Fountas and Gay Su Pinnell from *Sing a Song of Poetry, Grade 1*. Portsmouth, NH: Heinemann.

**SUGGESTION:** Invite children to find all of the *-ing* words. Create new verses using other verbs and different animals. Children may like to know that in this verse *pudding* means "sausage" (like a salami or hot dog) and hangs from a string.

fold here

# Sippity Sup

Sippity sup, sippity sup,

Bread and milk from a china cup,

Bread and milk

From a bright silver spoon,

Made of a piece

Of the bright silver moon!

Sippity sup, sippity sup,

Sippity, sippity, sup.

May be photocopied for classroom use. ©2018 by Irene C. Fountas and Gay Su Pinnell from *Sing a Song of Poetry, Grade 1.* Portsmouth, NH: Heinemann.

fold here

**SUGGESTION:** Have three or four children dramatize this poem, reciting lines while pretending to eat and drink with plastic cups and saucers. Ask the rest of the class to provide a layer of munching or slurping sounds or to softly repeat the words *sippity sup* throughout the recitation.

# Six Little Ducks

Six little ducks that I once knew,

Fat ducks, skinny ones, fair ones too,

But the one little duck with the feather on his back,

He led the others with his quack-quack-quack.


Down to the meadow they would go,

Wig-wag, wiggle-wag, to and fro,

But the one little duck with the feather on his back,

He led the others with his quack-quack-quack.

May be photocopied for classroom use. ©2018 by Irene C. Fountas and Gay Su Pinnell from *Sing a Song of Poetry, Grade 1*. Portsmouth, NH: Heinemann.

**SUGGESTION:** Children can pretend to be ducks as they sing this song. Alternatively, have six children be the ducks with a leader saying *quack-quack-quack*.

fold here

# Six Little Snowmen

Six little snowmen all made of snow,

Six little snowmen standing in a row.

Out came the sun and stayed all day,

One little snowman melted away.

Five little snowmen all made of snow.

May be photocopied for classroom use. ©2018 by Irene C. Fountas and Gay Su Pinnell from *Sing a Song of Poetry, Grade 1*. Portsmouth, NH: Heinemann.

fold here

**SUGGESTION:** This countdown poem begins with six and ends with zero as, one by one, the snowmen melt. Children can dramatize the poem by pretending to be snowmen melting onto the classroom floor.

# Sleep, Baby, Sleep!

Sleep, baby, sleep!

Thy father watches the sheep;

Thy mother is shaking the dreamland tree,

And down falls a little dream on thee:

Sleep, baby, sleep!


Sleep, baby, sleep!

The large stars are the sheep;

The wee stars are the lambs, I guess,

The fair moon is the shepherdess:

Sleep, baby, sleep!

May be photocopied for classroom use. ©2018 by Irene C. Fountas and Gay Su Pinnell from *Sing a Song of Poetry, Grade 1*. Portsmouth, NH: Heinemann.

**SUGGESTION:** Talking about some of the vocabulary in the poem will help children understand its use of metaphors. Have children whisper the final words. Some may not know that *thy* means "your" and *wee* means "little."

fold here

# Slip on Your Raincoat

Slip on your raincoat,

Pull on your galoshes;

Wading in puddles

Makes splishes and sploshes.

May be photocopied for classroom use. ©2018 by Irene C. Fountas and Gay Su Pinnell from *Sing a Song of Poetry, Grade 1*. Portsmouth, NH: Heinemann.

fold here

**SUGGESTION:** Compare this poem to "Little Raindrops" in this volume. Ask children how the poems are similar and how they are different. Talk about how *splishes* and *sploshes* sound like the noise you make splashing in puddles. Also, explain to children that *galoshes* means "rain boots."

# Slowly, Slowly

Slowly, slowly, very slowly,

Creeps the garden snail.

Slowly, slowly, very slowly,

Up the wooden rail.


Quickly, quickly, very quickly,

Runs the little mouse.

Quickly, quickly, very quickly,

'Round about the house.

May be photocopied for classroom use. ©2018 by Irene C. Fountas and Gay Su Pinnell from *Sing a Song of Poetry, Grade 1*. Portsmouth, NH: Heinemann.

**SUGGESTION:** Invite children to say the snail verse slowly and the mouse verse quickly. Let them create motions to go with the words of this poem. They will learn about opposites as they make the snail move slowly and the mouse run quickly. See if they can come up with other opposite words and movements.

fold here

# The Smile Song

I've got something in my pocket

That belongs upon my face.

I keep it very close at hand

In a most convenient place.


I think you wouldn't guess it

If you guessed a long, long while,

So I'll take it out and put it on.

It's a great big happy smile.

May be photocopied for classroom use. ©2018 by Irene C. Fountas and Gay Su Pinnell from *Sing a Song of Poetry, Grade 1*. Portsmouth, NH: Heinemann.

**SUGGESTION:** This is a great song to sing; its tune can be found on the Internet. The poem also presents itself as a riddle. Cover the title and the word *smile* on the last line. Then invite children to guess the answer. After the riddle is answered, children can pantomime holding something in a pocket during the first seven lines and then taking it out and putting it across the face, leaving a big smile.

# A Snail

A snail crept up the lily's stalk;

"How nice and smooth," said he;

"It's quite a pleasant evening walk,

And just the thing for me!"

May be photocopied for classroom use. ©2018 by Irene C. Fountas and Gay Su Pinnell from *Sing a Song of Poetry, Grade 1*. Portsmouth, NH: Heinemann.

**SUGGESTION:** Use this poem to call children's attention to quotation marks. Discuss the meaning of *crept*, and say the poem slowly as if the snail is creeping. Partners or small groups can take turns reading what the snail says. Pair this poem with "Slowly, Slowly" (also in this volume), featuring another creeping snail.

fold here

# Snow, Snow, Fly Away

Snow, snow,

Fly away

Over the hills

And far away.

May be photocopied for classroom use. ©2018 by Irene C. Fountas and Gay Su Pinnell from *Sing a Song of Poetry, Grade 1*. Portsmouth, NH: Heinemann.

**SUGGESTION:** Ask children what their favorite weather is. Have the whole class insert their weather words into the poem. Putting the poem in a pocket chart allows children to focus on the word substitutions and title changes. Or replace *snow, snow* with two blank spaces on a photocopied version, have children write their favorite weather words (*rain, wind, clouds,* etc.) in the spaces, and then take the poem home to share with family members.

# Snowman

This is a snowman as round as a ball.

He has two large eyes, but he's not very tall.

If the sun shines down on him today,

My jolly snowman will melt away.

May be photocopied for classroom use. ©2018 by Irene C. Fountas and Gay Su Pinnell from *Sing a Song of Poetry, Grade 1*. Portsmouth, NH: Heinemann.

SUGGESTION: Invite children to be snowmen. At the appropriate time, have them point to their eyes, point to the sun, and then fall slowly to the floor. Compare this poem to "Six Little Snowmen" (also in this volume).

fold here

# Soda Bread

Soda bread and soft bread,

Crazy bread and hard bread,

Loaf bread, cornbread,

Plain bread and biscuits.

May be photocopied for classroom use. ©2018 by Irene C. Fountas and Gay Su Pinnell from *Sing a Song of Poetry, Grade 1*. Portsmouth, NH: Heinemann.

**SUGGESTION:** Bread is a familiar concept for many children, but they may not know all the varieties. Make a class list (using interactive writing) of the different kinds of bread, including the breads in the poem as well as any others children generate: e.g., sourdough, wheat, oatmeal, and French. If needed, talk about the concept of a *loaf*.

# The Squirrel

Whisky, frisky,

Hippety hop,

Up he scrambles

To the treetop.

Whirly, furly,

What a tail!

Tall as a feather,

Broad as a sail!

Where's his supper?

In the shell.

Snappity, crackity—

Out it fell!

May be photocopied for classroom use. ©2018 by Irene C. Fountas and Gay Su Pinnell from *Sing a Song of Poetry, Grade 1*. Portsmouth, NH: Heinemann.

**SUGGESTION:** Invite children to pick out their favorite descriptive (onomatopoetic) words from the poem, such as *whisky, frisky, whirly, furly, snappity,* and *crackity*. Then ask them to play with altering their voice—high or low pitched, softer or louder. To share further images of a squirrel, read Beatrix Potter's *The Tale of Squirrel Nutkin* (1903). In this classic story, squirrels use their tails to help them sail across the water.

fold here

# Star Light, Star Bright

Star light, star bright,

First star I see tonight.

I wish I may, I wish I might

Have this wish I wish tonight.


Star sight, star height,

Second star I see in flight.

I wish this wish with all delight,

I wish this wish to be alright.

May be photocopied for classroom use. ©2018 by Irene C. Fountas and Gay Su Pinnell from *Sing a Song of Poetry, Grade 1*. Portsmouth, NH: Heinemann.

fold here

**SUGGESTION:** Children love telling their wishes and illustrating them after reciting the poem. Point out that every line has a rhyming word at the end; ask children to say *bright, tonight, might, height, flight, delight,* and *alright.*

# Stretch Up High

Stretch, stretch, way up high.

On your tiptoes, reach the sky.

See the bluebirds flying high.

Now bend down and touch your toes.

Now sway as the North Wind blows.

Waddle as the gander goes.

ACTIONS:

Stretch, stretch, way up high. [*reach arms upward*]

On your tiptoes, reach the sky. [*stand on tiptoes and reach*]

See the bluebirds flying high. [*wave hands*]

Now bend down and touch your toes. [*bend to touch toes*]

Now sway as the North Wind blows. [*move body back and forth*]

Waddle as the gander goes. [*walk in waddling motion*]

May be photocopied for classroom use. ©2018 by Irene C. Fountas and Gay Su Pinnell from *Sing a Song of Poetry, Grade 1*. Portsmouth, NH: Heinemann.

**SUGGESTION:** Have children say the poem and perform its accompanying actions. Point out the word *waddle*, and ask them what kind of animal they think *gander* is because it waddles. If they can't guess it, explain that a *gander* is "another name for a goose." This action rhyme is a good transition activity that will give children a moment of exercise before settling down again.

fold here

# A Sunshiny Shower

A sunshiny shower

Won't last half an hour.

May be photocopied for classroom use. ©2018 by Irene C. Fountas and Gay Su Pinnell from *Sing a Song of Poetry, Grade 1*. Portsmouth, NH: Heinemann.

**SUGGESTION:** Ask children if they have ever seen the sun out when it's raining. Discuss the concept of a short sunny shower, and ask them if they think the poem's short length is important given the poem's topic. Then invite children to talk about descriptive words, such as *sunshiny*. Work together to come up with some other expressive weather words: e.g., *rainy, messy, cloudy, muddy*, and so on. Create new weather couplets about a *cool wind, wet rain, soft snow*, etc.

# Swim Little Fish

Swim little fish

Swim around the pool.

Swim little fish

The water is cool.

Where's the little fish?

Where did he go?

There he is!

Splash!

May be photocopied for classroom use. ©2018 by Irene C. Fountas and Gay Su Pinnell from *Sing a Song of Poetry, Grade 1.* Portsmouth, NH: Heinemann.

**SUGGESTION:** Invite children to make swimming motions with their hands while saying the first four lines slowly. Then ask them to recite the fifth line faster while pantomiming looking for the fish before yelling *Splash!* and pretending to jump into water.

fold here

# Swim, Swan, Swim

Swan swam over the sea,

Swim, swan, swim!

Swan swam back again,

Well swum, swan!

May be photocopied for classroom use. ©2018 by Irene C. Fountas and Gay Su Pinnell from *Sing a Song of Poetry, Grade 1*. Portsmouth, NH: Heinemann.

fold here

**SUGGESTION:** This is another fun tongue twister that children can practice. Invite them to find all the *sw-* words. Help them to decide which of these are action words. Also help children stress particular words in order to convey the meaning.

# Ten Fat Sausages

Ten fat sausages sizzling in the pan,

Ten fat sausages sizzling in the pan.

One went POP! and another went BAM!

There were eight fat sausages sizzling in the pan.

**ADDITIONAL VERSES:**

Eight fat sausages sizzling in the pan,

Eight fat sausages sizzling in the pan.

One went POP! and another went BAM!

There were six fat sausages sizzling in the pan.

Six fat sausages sizzling in the pan,

Six fat sausages sizzling in the pan.

One went POP! and another went BAM!

There were four fat sausages sizzling in the pan.

Four fat sausages sizzling in the pan,

Four fat sausages sizzling in the pan.

One went POP! and another went BAM!

There were two fat sausages sizzling in the pan.

Two fat sausages sizzling in the pan,

Two fat sausages sizzling in the pan.

One went POP! and another went BAM!

There were no fat sausages sizzling in the pan.

May be photocopied for classroom use. ©2018 by Irene C. Fountas and Gay Su Pinnell from *Sing a Song of Poetry, Grade 1*. Portsmouth, NH: Heinemann.

fold here

**SUGGESTION:** There is a lot of action in this poem. That makes it interesting to illustrate as well as pantomime. *POP!* and *BAM!* are the parts children enjoy most when they perform the actions indicated. Emphasize the /s/ and /z/ of *sizzling* so children get the idea how these sausages sound when they cook. Start with ten fat sausages drawn on a whiteboard and subtract (erase) two at a time. Children enjoy coming up with the math equations for the disappearing sausages. This is also a good poem to revisit in a pocket chart.

# Thank You

My hands say thank you
With a clap, clap, clap.
My feet say thank you
With a tap, tap, tap.

Clap, clap, clap,
Tap, tap, tap.
I turn around,
Touch the ground,
And with a bow,
I say...Thank you, now.

ACTIONS:

My hands say thank you

With a clap, clap, clap. [*clap hands three times*]

My feet say thank you

With a tap, tap, tap. [*tap one toe three times*]

Clap, clap, clap, [*clap hands*]

Tap, tap, tap. [*tap toe*]

I turn around, [*turn around*]

Touch the ground, [*squat down to touch the ground*]

And with a bow, [*bow*]

I say...Thank you, now.

May be photocopied for classroom use. ©2018 by Irene C. Fountas and Gay Su Pinnell from *Sing a Song of Poetry, Grade 1*. Portsmouth, NH: Heinemann.

fold here

**SUGGESTION:** Have children say the rhyme with the motions. When they know the poem, children can locate or highlight the words with the *-ap* phonogram. This poem is good for locating high-frequency words.

# There Are Seven Days

There are seven days

There are seven days

There are seven days in a week.


Sunday, Monday,

Tuesday, Wednesday,

Thursday, Friday, Saturday.

May be photocopied for classroom use. ©2018 by Irene C. Fountas and Gay Su Pinnell from *Sing a Song of Poetry, Grade 1*. Portsmouth, NH: Heinemann.

fold here

**SUGGESTION:** Teach children to sing this poem to the tune of "Clementine." Repeat it several times until children associate the first day of the week with Sunday, the second day of the week with Monday, and so forth. Then ask them what day of the week it is today—name and number.

# There Once Was a Sow

There once was a sow

Who had three piglets,

Three little piglets had she.

And the old sow always went, "Umph,"

And the piglets went, "Wee, wee, wee."

May be photocopied for classroom use. ©2018 by Irene C. Fountas and Gay Su Pinnell from *Sing a Song of Poetry, Grade 1*. Portsmouth, NH: Heinemann.

**SUGGESTION:** Explain to children that a *sow* is "the mother pig" and *piglets* are "baby pigs." Then invite them to talk about other farm animals, their names, and the names of their babies: e.g., *cow* and *calf*.

# There Was an Old Lady Who Swallowed a Fly

There was an old lady who swallowed a fly.
I don't know why she swallowed the fly.
Perhaps she'll die.

There was an old lady who swallowed a spider
That wriggled and jiggled and tickled inside her.
She swallowed the spider to catch the fly.
I don't know why she swallowed the fly.

Perhaps she'll die.

**ADDITIONAL VERSES:**

There was an old lady who swallowed a bird.
How absurd! She swallowed a bird.

She swallowed the bird to catch . . .

There was an old lady who swallowed a cat.
Think of that! She swallowed a cat.

She swallowed the cat to catch . . .

There was an old lady who swallowed a dog.
What a hog! She swallowed a dog.

She swallowed the dog to catch . . .

There was an old lady who swallowed a goat.
It stuck in her throat! She swallowed a goat.

She swallowed the goat to catch . . .

There was an old lady who swallowed a horse.
She died, of course.

May be photocopied for classroom use. ©2018 by Irene C. Fountas and Gay Su Pinnell from *Sing a Song of Poetry, Grade 1*. Portsmouth, NH: Heinemann.

**SUGGESTION:** Invite children to make an old lady from an open paper bag by adding arms, legs, and a head. Let them draw and cut out all the things the old lady ate. Children will love to feed her, stuffing the bag while reciting the poem.

fold here

# There Was an Old Man of Peru

*by Edward Lear*

There was an old man of Peru

Who dreamed he was eating his shoe.

He woke in the night

In a terrible fright,

And found it was perfectly true.

May be photocopied for classroom use. ©2018 by Irene C. Fountas and Gay Su Pinnell from *Sing a Song of Poetry, Grade 1*. Portsmouth, NH: Heinemann.

fold here

**SUGGESTION**: Call attention to the rhymes at the ends of lines 1, 2, and 5, and then lines 3 and 4 by having children clap their hands or snap their fingers on the rhyming words. Once children are familiar with the poem's structure, have them substitute other people, places, and actions to create new limericks.

# There Was an Old Person of Ware

*by Edward Lear*

There was an old person of Ware,

Who rode on the back of a bear;

Then they asked, "Does it trot?"

He said, "Certainly not!

He's a Moppsikon Floppsikon bear!"

May be photocopied for classroom use. ©2018 by Irene C. Fountas and Gay Su Pinnell from *Sing a Song of Poetry, Grade 1*. Portsmouth, NH: Heinemann.

fold here

**SUGGESTION:** This is another entertaining limerick. Invite children to compare it to one of Edward Lear's other poems in this volume, "There Was an Old Man of Peru," both in number of rhymes and in each verse's rhythm. They will gradually internalize the form of a limerick.

# There's a Hole in the Middle of the Sea

There's a hole in the middle of the sea
There's a hole in the middle of the sea
There's a hole, there's a hole
There's a hole in the middle of the sea

There's a log in the hole in the middle of the sea
There's a log in the hole in the middle of the sea
There's a log, there's a log
There's a log in the hole in the middle of the sea

There's a bump on the log in the hole
In the middle of the sea
There's a bump on the log in the hole
In the middle of the sea
There's a bump, there's a bump
There's a bump on the log in the hole
In the middle of the sea

ADDITIONAL VERSES:

There's a frog on the bump on the log . . .

There's a fly on the frog on the bump on the log . . .

There's a wing on the fly on the frog . . .

There's a flea on the wing on the fly . . .

May be photocopied for classroom use. ©2018 by Irene C. Fountas and Gay Su Pinnell from *Sing a Song of Poetry, Grade 1*. Portsmouth, NH: Heinemann.

fold here

**SUGGESTION:** This cumulative rhyme can go on for many verses. The more characteristics you add, the more will be required of children's memories. Use judgment in adding verses, perhaps adding more over time.

# There's Music in a Hammer

There's music in a hammer.

There's music in a nail.

There's music in a kitty cat

When you step upon her tail.

May be photocopied for classroom use. ©2018 by Irene C. Fountas and Gay Su Pinnell from *Sing a Song of Poetry, Grade 1*. Portsmouth, NH: Heinemann.

fold here

**SUGGESTION:** Ask children to think about the kind of *music* that a cat might make when you step on her tail. Invite them to make the noises they think might occur—and remind them that this is only make-believe. Encourage children to talk about what is meant by the *music* (the beat) in a hammer or in a nail when you hit it.

# Thirty Days Has September

Thirty days has September,

April, June, and November.

February has twenty-eight alone

All the rest have thirty-one.

Excepting leap year, that's the time

When February's days are twenty-nine.

May be photocopied for classroom use. ©2018 by Irene C. Fountas and Gay Su Pinnell from *Sing a Song of Poetry, Grade 1*. Portsmouth, NH: Heinemann.

**SUGGESTION:** This traditional calendar poem will be a favorite that children turn to for years to come. Use it each new month as you check to see how many days there are. Test children's memories by asking how many days they think each new month has. Then turn the calendar's page and refer to the written poem for confirmation.

# This Little Hand

This little hand is a boy.

This little hand is his brother.

Together, they wash and they wash and they wash.

One hand washes the other.

May be photocopied for classroom use. ©2018 by Irene C. Fountas and Gay Su Pinnell from *Sing a Song of Poetry, Grade 1*. Portsmouth, NH: Heinemann.

**SUGGESTION:** Have children hold up one hand, then the other, and then pantomime washing their hands. Create a poetry chart and invite the class to illustrate the poem, drawing things like soap, soap bubbles, a sink, water, clean hands, etc. Then post the poetry chart near a classroom or bathroom sink.

fold here

# This Old Man

This old man,

He can shake,

Shake, shake, shake,

While baking a cake.

Knick-knack paddy-wack,

Give your dog a bone,

Shaking, shaking,

All the way home.

**ADDITIONAL VERSES:**

This old man,
He can kick,
Kick, kick, kick,
Just for a trick.
Knick-knack paddy-wack,
Give your dog a bone,
Kicking, kicking,
All the way home.

This old man,
He can twist,
Twist, twist, twist,
While shaking his fist.
Knick-knack paddy-wack,
Give your dog a bone,
Twisting, twisting,
All the way home.

**SUGGESTION:** This is a revised version of the traditional "This Old Man" song. It offers children the opportunity to notice rhyming words that have the same phonogram as well as what happens when you add *-ing* to words.

fold here

May be photocopied for classroom use. ©2018 by Irene C. Fountas and Gay Su Pinnell from *Sing a Song of Poetry, Grade 1.* Portsmouth, NH: Heinemann.

# Three Elephants

One elephant went out to play

Upon a spider's web one day.

He thought it such a tremendous stunt

That he called for another little elephant.


Two elephants went out to play

Upon a spider's web one day.

They thought it such a tremendous stunt

That they called for another little elephant.


Three elephants went out to play

Upon a spider's web one day.

The web went CREAK, the web went CRACK,

And all of a sudden they all ran back.

May be photocopied for classroom use. ©2018 by Irene C. Fountas and Gay Su Pinnell from *Sing a Song of Poetry, Grade 1*. Portsmouth, NH: Heinemann.

fold here

**SUGGESTION:** Children will enjoy being elephants and walking a spider-web tightrope. Just place a piece of yarn on the floor, and invite one, then two, and finally three children to be the elephants taking an imaginary trip as the rest of the class says the poem. When the web goes *CREAK* and *CRACK*, have the elephants all run back to the starting place. Substitute words such as *enormous* and *gigantic* for *tremendous* to expand children's vocabulary.

# Three Jolly Gentlemen

Three jolly gentlemen

In coats of red

Rode their horses

Up to bed.


Three jolly gentlemen

Snored till morn,

Their horses chomping

The golden corn.


Three jolly gentlemen

At break of day

Came clitter-clatter down the stairs

And galloped away.

May be photocopied for classroom use. ©2018 by Irene C. Fountas and Gay Su Pinnell from *Sing a Song of Poetry, Grade 1.* Portsmouth, NH: Heinemann.

fold here

**SUGGESTION:** Intive children to talk about what it might look like for people to ride horses up the stairs of a house. Help them notice that *clitter-clatter* is a way to represent the sound of horses' hooves. Ask children to give examples of the sounds other animals make while moving: e.g., a hummingbird's wings hum.

# Three Little Bugs

Three little bugs in a basket,

Hardly room for two.

One like Mary, one like Tom,

And one that looks like you.

May be photocopied for classroom use. ©2018 by Irene C. Fountas and Gay Su Pinnell from *Sing a Song of Poetry, Grade 1*. Portsmouth, NH: Heinemann.

**SUGGESTION:** This is a good poem for the start of the school year when children are still learning each other's names. Invite children to substitute names of classmates as they recite the poem. Create a *basket* by making a circle of yarn on the floor and putting children's names in the middle.

fold here

# Three Wise Men of Gotham

Three wise men of Gotham

Went to sea in a bowl;

If the bowl had been stronger,

My song would have been longer.

May be photocopied for classroom use. ©2018 by Irene C. Fountas and Gay Su Pinnell from *Sing a Song of Poetry, Grade 1*. Portsmouth, NH: Heinemann.

fold here

**SUGGESTION:** Ask children to puzzle out why this poem ends so abruptly. They will enjoy the joke when they figure out that the bowl sank. Invite them to make before and after pictures; this will help English language learners with tricky words such as *wise men* and *bowl*.

# Tick-Tock

"Tick-tock, tick-tock,

Tick-tock," says the clock.

Little boy, little girl,

Time to wash our hands.

May be photocopied for classroom use. ©2018 by Irene C. Fountas and Gay Su Pinnell from *Sing a Song of Poetry, Grade 1.* Portsmouth, NH: Heinemann.

fold here

**SUGGESTION:** Change this poem to fit any routine you have established in the classroom: e.g., *Time to read* or *Time for lunch*. Display this poem and any adaptations by the classroom activities or centers that are represented: e.g., by the sink where children wash their hands.

# Tingalayo

*Chorus*

    Tingalayo come, little donkey, come.

    Tingalayo come, little donkey, come.

Me donkey fast, me donkey slow,

Me donkey come and me donkey go.

*Chorus*

Me donkey hee, me donkey haw,

Me donkey sleep in a bed of straw.

*Chorus*

Me donkey dance, me donkey sing,

Me donkey wearin' a diamond ring.

*Chorus*

Me donkey swim, me donkey ski,

Me donkey dress elegantly.

May be photocopied for classroom use. ©2018 by Irene C. Fountas and Gay Su Pinnell from *Sing a Song of Poetry, Grade 1*. Portsmouth, NH: Heinemann.

fold here

**SUGGESTION:** Find this song's tune on the Internet (a Spanish version is also available). Then invite children to sing the song, repeating the chorus each time. Create new verses together and sing them as a class.

# A Tiny Seed

Tiny seed planted just right,

Not a breath of air, not a ray of light.

Rain falls slowly to and fro,

And now the seed begins to grow.


Slowly reaching for the light,

With all its energy, all its might.

The little seed's work is almost done,

To grow up tall and face the sun.

May be photocopied for classroom use. ©2018 by Irene C. Fountas and Gay Su Pinnell from *Sing a Song of Poetry, Grade 1*. Portsmouth, NH: Heinemann.

**SUGGESTION:** This is a good transitioning poem to perform between activities. Have children roll up in a ball and then start to unfold as the seed begins to grow. At the end of the poem, invite them to stand up tall and stretch their arms.

fold here

# To Bed, to Bed

To bed, to bed,

Says sleepy-head.

Tarry a while,

Says Slow.

Put on the pan,

Says Greedy Nan,

We'll sup before we go.

May be photocopied for classroom use. ©2018 by Irene C. Fountas and Gay Su Pinnell from *Sing a Song of Poetry, Grade 1*. Portsmouth, NH: Heinemann.

**SUGGESTION:** Talk with children about the words *tarry*, meaning "stay," and *sup*, meaning "to eat supper." Who do they think *Slow* and *Greedy Nan* are?

# Tom, Tom, the Piper's Son

Tom, he was a piper's son,

He learned to play when he was young;

But the only tune that he could play

Was "Over the Hills and Far Away."


Now Tom with his pipe made such a noise,

That he pleased all the girls and boys;

And they stopped to hear him play

"Over the Hills and Far Away."

May be photocopied for classroom use. ©2018 by Irene C. Fountas and Gay Su Pinnell from *Sing a Song of Poetry, Grade 1*. Portsmouth, NH: Heinemann.

fold here

**SUGGESTION:** Discuss the idea of a *pipe* being a musical instrument such as a flute, a clarinet, or a recorder. Ask children to listen to you read the poem and to pick out the rhyming words. Then invite them to clap the rhyming words.

# Traffic Safety

Red light says stop.

Green light says go.

Yellow says be careful,

You'd better go slow.


When I reach a crossing place,

To left and right I turn my face.

And then I walk, not run, across the street,

And use my head to guide my feet.

May be photocopied for classroom use. ©2018 by Irene C. Fountas and Gay Su Pinnell from *Sing a Song of Poetry, Grade 1*. Portsmouth, NH: Heinemann.

fold here

**SUGGESTION:** Assign select children to read *stop, go,* and *be careful, you'd better go slow* while performing actions they think best complement the words. Invite the rest of the class to recite the second stanza while also performing actions that match the words: e.g., turning their faces to the left and right.

# Tweedledum and Tweedledee

Tweedledum and Tweedledee

Were set to have a battle,

For Tweedledum said Tweedledee

Had tried to tell a tattle.


Just then flew by a monstrous crow,

Who wasn't too polite.

It frightened both the heroes so,

They quite forgot to fight.

May be photocopied for classroom use. ©2018 by Irene C. Fountas and Gay Su Pinnell from *Sing a Song of Poetry, Grade 1*. Portsmouth, NH: Heinemann.

fold here

**SUGGESTION:** This humorous poem will be fun and relatable to firstgraders, especially since tattling is something they often do or try not to do. Have half the class read the first stanza and the other half read the second stanza. Also ask children if they recognize the characters Tweedledum and Tweedledee. They might know them from Lewis Carroll's *Through the Looking-Glass and What Alice Found There* (1871). If not, read an excerpt about Tweedledum and Tweedledee from this classic nonsense story.

# Twenty White Horses

Twenty white horses

Upon a red hill;

Now they tramp,

Now they chomp,

Now they stand still.

May be photocopied for classroom use. ©2018 by Irene C. Fountas and Gay Su Pinnell from *Sing a Song of Poetry, Grade 1*. Portsmouth, NH: Heinemann.

fold here

**SUGGESTION:** Children enjoy riddles and wordplay. Let them take the lead in discovering the meaning of *red hill*, *tramp*, and *chomp*. They will love discovering that the *white horses* are teeth!

# Two Cats of Kilkenny

There once were two cats of Kilkenny.

Each thought there was one cat too many;

So they fought and they fit,

And they scratched and they bit,

Till, excepting their nails,

And the tips of their tails,

Instead of two cats, there weren't any.

May be photocopied for classroom use. ©2018 by Irene C. Fountas and Gay Su Pinnell from *Sing a Song of Poetry, Grade 1*. Portsmouth, NH: Heinemann.

**SUGGESTION:** This is a good poem to turn into prose. Invite children to dictate to you a concise retelling: e.g., Two cats fought each other until there wasn't anything left of them. Also, ask them to talk about the poem's lesson.

fold here

# Two Crows

There were two crows sat on a stone,

Fal-de-ral, fal-de-ral.

One flew away and there was one,

Fal-de-ral, fal-de-ral.

The other seeing his neighbor gone,

Fal-de-ral, fal-de-ral.

He flew away and then there were none,

Fal-de-ral, fal-de-ral.

May be photocopied for classroom use. ©2018 by Irene C. Fountas and Gay Su Pinnell from *Sing a Song of Poetry, Grade 1.* Portsmouth, NH: Heinemann.

fold here

**SUGGESTION:** When you say *fal-de-ral* the first time, say it quickly. Then pace the second *fal-de-ral* more deliberately and slowly. Children will understand that the first, third, fifth, and seventh lines really tell a story and that *fal-de-ral* is added to make the poem more rhythmic and engaging.

# Two Little Dogs

Two little dogs sat by the fire

In a basket of coal dust.

Says one little dog to the other little dog,

If you don't speak, then I must.

May be photocopied for classroom use. ©2018 by Irene C. Fountas and Gay Su Pinnell from *Sing a Song of Poetry, Grade 1*. Portsmouth, NH: Heinemann.

**SUGGESTION:** Explain to children that people sometimes make fires with *coal*, which are "black rocks that burn but leave dust." The little dogs are sitting in a coal basket by the fire. Compare the words *dust* and *must*.

fold here

# Up in the Green Orchard

Up in the green orchard there is a green tree,

The finest of pippins that you may see.

The apples are ripe and ready to fall,

And Robin and Richard shall gather them all.

May be photocopied for classroom use. ©2018 by Irene C. Fountas and Gay Su Pinnell from *Sing a Song of Poetry, Grade 1*. Portsmouth, NH: Heinemann.

fold here

**SUGGESTION:** Once children know that *pippins* are green apples, they'll understand why this piece of land is called *the green orchard*. Substitute names of children in class for *Robin* and *Richard*. Substitute other fruit (*apricots, peaches, cherries*) for *pippins*, and change the color in the name of the orchard accordingly.

# The Vowel Song

The vowels of the alphabet

I know them all by name, oh!

a–e–i–o–u

a–e–i–o–u

a–e–i–o–u

I know them all by name, oh!

May be photocopied for classroom use. ©2018 by Irene C. Fountas and Gay Su Pinnell from *Sing a Song of Poetry, Grade 1*. Portsmouth, NH: Heinemann.

**SUGGESTION:** Invite children to sing this poem to the tune of "B–i–n–g–o." Have them repeat it five more times. Each time, instruct children to insert a clap for a vowel.

fold here

# Way Down South

Way down south where bananas grow,

A grasshopper stepped on an elephant's toe.

The elephant said, with tears in his eyes,

"Pick on somebody your own size."

May be photocopied for classroom use. ©2018 by Irene C. Fountas and Gay Su Pinnell from *Sing a Song of Poetry, Grade 1*. Portsmouth, NH: Heinemann.

fold here

**SUGGESTION:** Invite children to talk about what makes this poem funny. As children imagine the size of an elephant and the size of a grasshopper, they will realize the poem's contrasting humor.

# What Animals Say

Bow-wow, says the dog;
Mew, mew, says the cat;
Grunt, grunt, says the hog;
And squeak, says the rat.

Chirp, chirp, says the sparrow;
Caw, caw, says the crow;
Quack, quack, says the duck;
What cuckoos say, you know.

With sparrows and cuckoos,
With rats and dogs,
With ducks and crows,
With cats and hogs,

A fine song I've made,
To please you, my dear;
And if it's well sung,
'Twill be charming to hear.

May be photocopied for classroom use. ©2018 by Irene C. Fountas and Gay Su Pinnell from *Sing a Song of Poetry, Grade 1*. Portsmouth, NH: Heinemann.

**SUGGESTION:** After reading the poem as a group, invite children to make paper masks of their favorite animal from the poem. Then group children by their favorite animals and invite them to put on their paper masks. Have the class perform the first three stanzas of the poem, limiting each animal group to its respective lines; in stanza three, two groups of animals will recite their respective lines together. Read the last stanza to the class, but pause before the final line. On cue, invite all children to sing their animal sounds. Afterwards, in response, read to them the last line of the poem.

fold here

# What Do You See?

What do you see?

A pig in a tree.

Where's your cat?

Under my hat.

How do you know?

He licked my toe.

May be photocopied for classroom use. ©2018 by Irene C. Fountas and Gay Su Pinnell from *Sing a Song of Poetry, Grade 1*. Portsmouth, NH: Heinemann.

**SUGGESTION:** Children love nonsense poems like this one and enjoy creating more: e.g., *What can you do? / Swim in a shoe. / Where's your chair? / Under the bear.* Children's own rhymes and illustrations make a great bulletin board display or class book. These verses also give English language learners practice using difficult words such as *over,* *under, behind,* and *in front of.*

# What's Your Name?

What's your name?

Puddin Tame.

Ask me again

And I'll tell you the same.

Where do you live?

In a sieve.

What's your number?

Cucumber!

May be photocopied for classroom use. ©2018 by Irene C. Fountas and Gay Su Pinnell from *Sing a Song of Poetry, Grade 1.* Portsmouth, NH: Heinemann.

**SUGGESTION:** Children can act out this poem by having half the group read the questions and the other half read the answers. This is a good poem to call children's attention to punctuation.

fold here

# When You and I Grow Up

*by Kate Greenaway*

When you and I

Grow up—Polly—

I mean that you and me,

Shall go sailing in a big ship

Right over all the sea.

We'll wait till we are older,

For if we went today,

You know that we might lose ourselves,

And never find the way.

May be photocopied for classroom use. ©2018 by Irene C. Fountas and Gay Su Pinnell from *Sing a Song of Poetry, Grade 1.* Portsmouth, NH: Heinemann.

**SUGGESTION:** This poem inspires children to think about who they want to grow up to be and what they want to do. Recite the poem together as a class until it is familiar. Then have children partner up and recite the poem to each other, substituting *Polly* for their partner's name. Have them ask their partners who they want to grow up to be and what they want to do. Invite children to illustrate their partners' responses. Children can then present to the class what they learned about their classmates.

# Where Do You Wear Your Ears?

Where do you wear your ears?

Underneath your hat?

Where do you wear your ears?

Yes ma'am, just like that.

Where do you wear your ears?

Say where, you sweet, sweet child.

Where do you wear your ears?

On both ends of my smile!

May be photocopied for classroom use. ©2018 by Irene C. Fountas and Gay Su Pinnell from *Sing a Song of Poetry, Grade 1*. Portsmouth, NH: Heinemann.

**SUGGESTION:** Once children are familiar with the poem, ask them to replace *ears* and *smile* with other parts of the face or body: e.g., *eyes, mouth, nose, hair, arms, legs,* and *feet.* They can also replace *hat* with a different article of clothing. Invite children to be as creative and silly as their imaginations will allow. Then have them pick their favorite adaptations to illustrate accordingly.

fold here

# Where, Oh, Where Has My Little Dog Gone?

Where, oh, where has my little dog gone?

Where, oh, where can he be?

With his ears cut short and his tail cut long,

Oh, where, oh, where can he be?

May be photocopied for classroom use. ©2018 by Irene C. Fountas and Gay Su Pinnell from *Sing a Song of Poetry, Grade 1.* Portsmouth, NH: Heinemann.

**SUGGESTION:** Firstgraders can envision and describe the missing pet. Assign one-third of the children to read each of the first three lines and then have everyone read the final line. Use interactive writing to make a lost dog poster. Note that this poem's topic may be sensitive to children who have experienced the loss of a pet or have a pet who is missing.

# Whose Little Pigs

Whose little pigs are these, these, these?

Whose little pigs are these?

They are Roger the cook's;

I know by their looks.

I found them among my peas.

May be photocopied for classroom use. ©2018 by Irene C. Fountas and Gay Su Pinnell from *Sing a Song of Poetry, Grade 1*. Portsmouth, NH: Heinemann.

**SUGGESTION:** Children will enjoy this poem and may substitute other animal names for *pigs* without changing the poem in any other way. Do, however, call their attention to the title change. Also call attention to the word *whose*, and discuss why this word means the pigs belong to someone.

fold here

# Wibbleton to Wobbleton

From Wibbleton to Wobbleton is fifteen miles.

From Wobbleton to Wibbleton is fifteen miles.

From Wibbleton to Wobbleton,

From Wobbleton to Wibbleton,

From Wibbleton to Wobbleton is fifteen miles.

May be photocopied for classroom use. ©2018 by Irene C. Fountas and Gay Su Pinnell from *Sing a Song of Poetry, Grade 1*. Portsmouth, NH: Heinemann.

fold here

**SUGGESTION:** This rhythmic verse is fun for children to recite; it's a bit of a tongue twister, so it may take multiple attempts to learn. Slow down when you say *fifteen miles*. Talk with children about this rhyme describing a journey from town to town. After children know the rhyme, call attention to the double consonants.

# Wiggly Woo

There's a worm at the bottom of the garden,

And his name is Wiggly Woo.

There's a worm at the bottom of the garden

And all that he can do

Is wiggle all night

And wiggle all day.

Whatever else the people say,

There's a worm at the bottom of the garden

And his name is Wiggly Woo.

May be photocopied for classroom use. ©2018 by Irene C. Fountas and Gay Su Pinnell from *Sing a Song of Poetry, Grade 1*. Portsmouth, NH: Heinemann.

**SUGGESTION:** Invite children to make wiggling motions with their hands every time they recite a word that starts with the letter *w*. After they learn the rhyme, call attention to double consonants and vowels.

fold here

# Willy Boy, Willy Boy

"Willy boy, Willy boy, where are you going?

I'll go with you, if I may."

"I'm going to the meadow to see them a-mowing;

I'm going to help them make hay."

May be photocopied for classroom use. ©2018 by Irene C. Fountas and Gay Su Pinnell from *Sing a Song of Poetry, Grade 1*. Portsmouth, NH: Heinemann.

fold here   **SUGGESTION:** Have half the children read the first two lines and have the rest reply by reading the last two. Then invite them to talk about where *hay* is made and what else they might find there: e.g., farm animals, tractors, and barns.

# The Wind

I can blow like the wind.

I can bring the rain.

When I blow very softly,

I can whisper my name.

May be photocopied for classroom use. ©2018 by Irene C. Fountas and Gay Su Pinnell from *Sing a Song of Poetry, Grade 1*. Portsmouth, NH: Heinemann.

**SUGGESTION:** Invite children to create the sounds of wind and rain and then whisper their names on cue.

fold here

# A Wise Old Owl

*by E. H. Richards*

A wise old owl lived in an oak.

The more he saw, the less he spoke;

The less he spoke, the more he heard.

Why can't we all be like that wise old bird?

May be photocopied for classroom use. ©2018 by Irene C. Fountas and Gay Su Pinnell from *Sing a Song of Poetry, Grade 1*. Portsmouth, NH: Heinemann.

fold here

**SUGGESTION:** After an initial reading of the poem, ask for three volunteers to pantomime actions as the class recites: e.g., using a hand to shade eyes and looking from side to side; covering the mouth so as not to speak; and cupping both hands behind ears. While reciting the last line, invite each child to raise both arms in question. Then encourage a discussion about speaking and listening within a group.

# References

Archambault, John, and David Plummer. 1998. *I Love the Mountains: A Traditional Song.* Silver Burdett Press.

Carroll, Lewis. 1871. *Through the Looking-Glass and What Alice Found There.* London, England: Macmillan Children's Books, an imprint of Macmillan Publishers.

Carroll, Lewis. 1865. *Alice's Adventures in Wonderland.* London, England: Macmillan Children's Books, an imprint of Macmillan Publishers.

Demarest, Chris. 2000. *Firefighters A to Z.* New York, NY: Margaret K. McElderry Books, an imprint of Simon & Schuster Children's Publishing Division, Simon & Schuster.

Ehlert, Lois. 1991. *Red Leaf, Yellow Leaf.* New York, NY: Houghton Mifflin Harcourt Books for Young Readers, an imprint of Houghton Mifflin Harcourt Books for Young Readers Division, Houghton Mifflin Harcourt.

Forest, Heather. 2006. *The Little Red Hen: An Old Fable.* Little Rock, AR: August House LittleFolk. From *Fountas & Pinnell Classroom™ Interactive Read-Aloud Collection, Grade 1.* © 2018 by Irene C. Fountas and Gay Su Pinnell. Portsmouth, NH: Heinemann.

Fountas, Irene C., and Gay Su Pinnell. 2018. *Fountas & Pinnell Classroom™ Interactive Read-Aloud Collection, Grade 1.* Portsmouth, NH: Heinemann.

———. 2018. *Fountas & Pinnell Classroom™ Shared Reading Collection, Grade 1.* Portsmouth, NH: Heinemann.

———. 2018. *Fountas & Pinnell Phonics, Spelling, and Word Study Lessons, Grade 1.* Portsmouth, NH: Heinemann.

———. 2017. *Guided Reading: Responsive Teaching Across the Grades,* Second Edition. Portsmouth, NH: Heinemann.

Hale, Sarah. 1990. *Mary Had a Little Lamb.* New York, NY: Scholastic Inc.

Harley, Bill. 1996. *Sitting Down to Eat.* Little Rock, AR: August House LittleFolk. From *Fountas & Pinnell Classroom™ Interactive Read-Aloud Collection, Grade 1.* © 2018 by Irene C. Fountas and Gay Su Pinnell. Portsmouth, NH: Heinemann.

Hoberman, Mary Ann. 1997. *One of Each.* New York, NY: Little, Brown Books for Young Readers, an imprint of Hachette Book Group. From *Fountas & Pinnell Classroom™ Interactive Read-Aloud Collection, Grade 1.* © 2018 by Irene C. Fountas and Gay Su Pinnell. Portsmouth, NH: Heinemann.

Langstaff, John. 2001. *Jackfish and More Songs for Singing Children.* Watertown, MA: Revels Records.

———. 1996. *Songs for Singing Children.* Watertown, MA: Revels Records.

Lindbergh, Reeve. 1990. *The Day the Goose Got Loose*. New York, NY: Dial Books for Young Readers, an imprint of Penguin Young Readers Group, Penguin Random House. From *Fountas & Pinnell Classroom™ Interactive Read-Aloud Collection, Grade 1*. © 2018 by Irene C. Fountas and Gay Su Pinnell. Portsmouth, NH: Heinemann.

Lord, John Vernon, and Janet Burroway. 2000. *The Giant Jam Sandwich*. New York, NY: Houghton Mifflin Harcourt Books for Young Readers, an imprint of Houghton Mifflin Harcourt Books for Young Readers Division, Houghton Mifflin Harcourt. From *Fountas & Pinnell Classroom™ Interactive Read-Aloud Collection, Grade 1*. © 2018 by Irene C. Fountas and Gay Su Pinnell. Portsmouth, NH: Heinemann

McCarrier, Andrea, Gay Su Pinnell, and Irene C. Fountas. 2000. *Interactive Writing: How Language and Literacy Come Together, K–2*. Portsmouth, NH: Heinemann.

McQueen, Lucinda. 1985. *The Little Red Hen*. New York, NY: Scholastic, Inc. From *Fountas & Pinnell Classroom™ Interactive Read-Aloud Collection, Grade 1*. © 2018 by Irene C. Fountas and Gay Su Pinnell. Portsmouth, NH: Heinemann.

Morris, Norma. *Coming Around the Mountain*. From *Fountas & Pinnell Classroom™ Shared Reading Collection, Grade 1*. © 2018 by Irene C. Fountas and Gay Su Pinnell. Portsmouth, NH: Heinemann.

Opie, Iona, and Rosemary Wells. 1997. *Little Boy Blue*. Somerville, MA: Candlewick Press.

Peek, Merle. 1985. *Mary Wore Her Red Dress and Henry Wore His Green Sneakers*. New York, NY: Clarion Books, an imprint of Houghton Mifflin Harcourt Books for Young Readers Division, Houghton Mifflin Harcourt.

Pinnell, Gay Su, and Irene C. Fountas. 1998. *Word Matters: Teaching Phonics and Spelling in the Reading/Writing Classroom*. Portsmouth, NH: Heinemann.

Potter, Beatrix. 1903. *The Tale of Squirrel Nutkin*. London, England: Penguin Books, an imprint of Penguin Random House Children's, Penguin Random House UK.

Trapani, Iza. 2000. *Shoo Fly!* Watertown, MA: Charlesbridge.

Weeks, Sarah. 1988. *Mrs. McNosh Hangs Up Her Wash*. New York, NY: HarperTrophy, an imprint of HarperCollins Publishers. From *Fountas & Pinnell Classroom™ Interactive Read-Aloud Collection, Grade 1*. © 2018 by Irene C. Fountas and Gay Su Pinnell. Portsmouth, NH: Heinemann.